ADULT ONLY
PRACTICAL
JOKES

Guaranteed to make you giggle!

HINKLER
BOOKS

Joke Compilation: Scribblers and Writers
Cover Design: Sam Grimmer
Illustrations: John Shakespeare
Editor: Jasmine Chan
Typesetting: Midland Typesetters, Maryborough, Vic, Australia

 Adults Only Practical Jokes
First published in 2004 by Hinkler Books Pty Ltd
45-55 Fairchild Street
Heatherton VIC 3202 Australia
www.hinklerbooks.com.au

10 9 8 7 6 5 4
10 09 08 07

ISBN 1 7412 1658 3

Printed and bound in China

INTRODUCTION

Laughing can help you feel happier and be healthier. Jokes help you to make a day, a place or a situation more bearable. They make you laugh and they should make the people around you laugh as well.

They can help people to relax and to enjoy the moment.

However, it is important—especially with practical jokes—to know when to stop and to come in out of the rain.

Always remember:

- A practical joke isn't funny if it makes the person upon whom you are playing it feel bad.
- Don't keep the joke going for so long that everybody around you is bored and wishing that you would just go away.
- Don't play jokes that might backfire and cause injury or damage.

The scope of the practical joke is only limited by the prankster's imagination and the amount of knowledge and education possessed by the person on whom the joke is being played.

As mass communication becomes more sophisticated and as more people around the world have easy access to computers and libraries, it is becoming increasingly more difficult to trick whole populations as was done in the past:

In 1957, a British television show convinced viewers that spaghetti grew on spaghetti trees. People believed them because, at that time, in Britain, the diet was different than it is today and very few people had any experience eating spaghetti. It was foreign to them.

ADULTS ONLY PRACTICAL JOKES

In 1985, an American sports magazine claimed that a New York baseball team was trying to sign up a new pitcher who could throw a ball much faster than anyone had ever thrown one before. The problem was that the pitcher could not decide whether he wanted to play baseball or play the French horn.

In 1989, the British businessman Richard Branson, who went on to launch Virgin Airlines, flew a hot-air balloon that looked like a flying saucer over London. The city buzzed with gossip that the aliens had landed.

A newspaper in Illinois once ran a story advising consumers that Illinois Bell, the telephone company, would, on a particular day, be 'blowing the dust out of the phone lines', and that, on that day, all phone owners should cover the earpiece of their phones with a bag to catch the dust.

Bell made them print a retraction, after receiving numerous calls asking what sort of bag to use.

In New York, just after World War II, college students, masquerading as workmen, dug a large hole in the street and then went off and left it. It was days before anybody realised something was wrong and traffic was a disaster until the street department patched the hole.

This joke was taken even further when the jokers observed the real workmen digging up the street and reported it to the police, saying that college students were at it again and were once more wrecking the street as a joke.

The police thanked the tipster and headed for the dig.

In the meantime the jokers approached the workmen and told them that the college students would be dressing up as policemen and that they would be arriving soon and would be trying to tell the workmen to stop what they were doing.

So, of course, when the police arrived, there was real confusion all round and the practical jokers had lots to laugh about.

Another famous joke was played when a college student returned to his room to find a bucket of water amateurishly balanced above the door, ready to fall on him when he opened the door.

He gently lifted the bucket down from the door and walked over to the sink and emptied it.

Too bad that the practical jokers had planned it that way—they had removed the drain pipe from the sink!

Then there was the American newspaper that claimed that the Wisconsin State Capitol Building had collapsed after several explosions. The newspaper included a picture of the building with its dome falling off.

This was in 1933, long before computers could fake photographs.

George Adamski, an inveterate practical joker, fooled many people worldwide.

In 1952, he made strange footsteps in the sand and convinced many people that they were the footprints of aliens.

He made up stories about how he was taken by aliens to the other side of the Moon where he saw many wonderful things about life there and on other planets.

He described the mother ship and the UFOs and the strange little people who rode in them.

There was no internet in those days, men hadn't flown into outer space and science still had many things to learn and so, his strange tales were widely believed.

He was a successful practical jokester because he tricked people about something that they didn't know much about.

But he had an excellent imagination!

Then there was Larry Walters, a truck driver from Los Angeles.

He tied 45 weather balloons to his aluminium lawn chair and floated up 11,000 feet above his back yard.

He didn't go unprepared.

He took with him a parachute, a CB radio, a six-pack, peanut butter and jelly sandwiches and a gun to shoot out the balloons when he decided it was time to return.

Not forgetting this great story—perhaps an urban legend—that is regularly told by somebody who knows somebody who knows somebody who swears it happened.

Two university students made up a concoction of all kinds of left-over food, semi-pureed it in a blender and filled a hot water bottle with it.

One of them took the hot water bottle, taped it to his stomach inside his shirt and put a short piece of hose into the top so that it came up to the front of his shirt collar, but was not visible.

They went to a local pub and sat at the bar, acting already slightly intoxicated.

After having a couple of beers, the guy with the hot water bottle starts saying that he is feeling sick. He 'coughed' very loudly to attract attention.

Then he leans over the bar, coughing and pretending to throw up and squirts the contents of the hot water bottle all over the bar.

This caused the patrons to move away from him, all except his mate, who calmly pulls a fork out of his coat pocket and begins to *eat* the stuff.

This may or may not be true, but it makes a good story.

In recent times, the Cyber Practical Joke has appeared on the scene, whereby large numbers of people can take part, as they have access to a computer and so can be contacted easily.

An example of this type of joke happened this year in Melbourne.

An SMS message went out to all and sundry inviting them to turn up at the Flinders Street Railway Station in the centre of the city and the main commuting point for its workers.

All they were told was that they would need to be at the gathering point at 4.49 pm precisely. Nothing else was divulged.

About 500 people turned up. They were each given a yellow plastic glove and told to keep it concealed until the clock chimed 5.00 pm. They were to then take the glove, put it on the right hand and to point at the sky, to hold this pose until the clock ceased to chime, put the gloved hand in their pocket and to walk away.

They dutifully did this and the puzzled commuters of Melbourne, walking past at that moment, went home that night to tell their families at dinner time the strange phenomenon that occurred on the way home.

Aclassic practical prank supposedly happened in the '60s—a pre-ATM time when deposit slips at a bank were laid out in trays for customers to fill in their own details before depositing money.

The banks were just beginning to imprint each person's account number on deposit slips, but they were not very common.

A man opened an account; deposited some money and then he left his own deposit slips in the trays with the ones that were used by everybody.

He did this in several different branches and then just before the end of the month, when the monthly statements came out and people may have realised that something was wrong, he walked into the bank and withdrew all of the funds that everybody had so very kindly deposited into his account.

They never saw him again.

Overall, the clever practical joke has to be imaginative, funny and believable.

A joke is not funny if it makes another person feel bad.

Some of the jokes in this book have the potential to be hurtful if they are played with too heavy a hand.

That is up to the prankster.

Play the joke so that everyone can laugh, not just the person playing it.

ADULTS ONLY PRACTICAL JOKES

A good practical joke gives everyone involved a good belly laugh.

Remember that laughter is the best medicine and that it is easier to have friends than enemies.

Keep the jokes funny.

ANSWERING MACHINE ANSWERS

The phone answering machine gives you a great opportunity to leave people puzzled, astounded or outraged.

Leave some of these on the machine.

Better still, not on *your* machine—sneak in and put them on your friend's when he doesn't know it!

A is for academics, B is for beer.
One of those reasons is why we're not here. So, leave a message.

Hello. We're not here right now—we prefer to go out and socialise with intelligent people, not dumb bastards like you. Leave a message if you really have to.

Hello. If it's anyone important, leave a message. If it's Deborah, the monthly child payment is in the mail. But I'm still not convinced the kid's mine. I'm ready for a DNA anytime. I betcha it's that prick Barry, isn't it? It was him that fathered the kid, hey, wasn't? Huh?

Hi. This is Greg. If you are the gas company, I already sent the money. If you are my parents, please send money. If you are the credit union, you didn't lend me enough money. If you are my friends, you owe me money. If you are a female, don't worry, I have plenty of money.

Hi, I'm not home right now, but my answering machine is, so you can talk to it instead. It's probably smarter than you. Wait for the beep.

Hello. I am Jim's answering machine. What are you?

How dare you ring this number and expect someone to be here! We have places to go, people to see, hamburgers to eat . . .

Hello! If you leave a message, I'll call you soon. If you leave a 'sexy' message, I'll call you sooner!

Hi. I go out to avoid people like you ringing up all the time and whinging. Get a life.

Hi! Derek the Geek's answering machine is broken. This is his refrigerator. Please speak very slowly and I'll stick your message to myself with one of these magnets.

Hello, you are talking to a machine. I am capable of receiving messages. My owners do not need aluminium cladding, double-glazed windows or a hot tub in western red cedar. And their carpets are clean. They give to charity through their office and do not need their picture taken. If you're still with me, leave your name and number and they will get back to you.

This is not an answering machine—this is a telepathic thought-recording device. After the tone, think about your name, your number and your reason for calling and I'll think about returning your call.

Hi. I'm probably home; I'm just avoiding someone I don't like. Leave me a message and if I don't call back, it's you.

Hi, this is George. I'm sorry I can't answer the phone right now. Leave a message and then wait by your phone until I call you back.

If you are a burglar, then we're at home cleaning our weapons of mass destruction right now and can't come to the phone. Otherwise, we probably aren't home and it's safe to leave a message.

Please leave a message. However, you have the right to remain silent. Everything you say will be recorded and will be used by us.

APRIL FOOL'S DAY

A GREAT DAY FOR PRACTICAL JOKES

Why do we have April Fool's Day?

Until the 16th century, the French used to celebrate the New Year on the first day of spring; that is, 1 April.

However in 1562, Pope Gregory changed the calendar to the one we use today, where the first day of the New Year is on 1 January.

Many people remained ignorant of the new calendar and so they continued to celebrate the New Year on 1 April.

Because of their ignorance they were considered April 'fools' and people played jokes on them.

April Fools' Day is celebrated in different ways in different parts of the world. In France, 1 April is called Poisson d'Avril—which means April Fish.

Children tape a paper fish to their friends' backs and when the young 'fool' finds out, the prankster yells 'Poisson d'Avril!' or April Fish!

In England, tricks can only be played in the morning.

If a trick is played on you, you are a 'noodle'.

In Scotland, April Fool's Day is celebrated over two days. On the first day you can be made an 'April gowk', which is another name for a cuckoo.

The second day is devoted to pranks involving the bottom and is called Taily Day.

In Portugal, April Fool's is celebrated on the Sunday and Monday before Lent.

Pranksters usually throw flour at their friends.

APRIL FOOL'S DAY

It is traditional to play practical jokes on people on April 1—April Fool's Day. Mums and Dads seem to get a real kick out of playing jokes on their children on this day and then laughing and saying, 'Gotcha, you big April Fool.'

But there's no reason that kids can't join in the fun; it just takes a bit of thinking ahead and a little preparation.

April Fool's practical jokes should be done in good fun and not meant to harm anyone. The best jokes are the clever ones where everyone laughs, especially the person who had the joke played on them.

To play a good April Fool's joke you really need to know the person you are playing it against and then you can do something that really makes everyone laugh.

For example, if you have a teenage brother who hates to get out of bed in the morning, you could knock on his door and tell him that the girl he adores from afar from up the street is on the telephone and would like to speak to him. Enjoy seeing him spring out of bed and fly downstairs in his jocks only to be told, 'April Fool!'

Remember to keep well out of range to avoid his anger.

April Fool's Day jokes range from the simple ('Your shoe is untied!'), to the very elaborate ones that are played by the radio and TV networks and which fool whole cities.

APRIL FOOL'S DAY

Take some gummy worms and carefully poke them into fresh apples.

Offer the wormy apples for lunch and leave a few apples on the table for friends and family members to snack on.

They will know that you have made them April Fools.

SPRAY THAT AGAIN

If you have a sink with a sprayer, put a rubber band around the handle when nobody's looking.

This automatically keeps the nozzle in spray-mode.

Make sure the nozzle is pointing up and outward.

The next person to use the sink will get a splash!

Hang around and tell him/her that he/she is an April Fool.

SEE MY GARDEN GROW

Make a brightly coloured papier-maché mushroom or get some artificial flowers and plant them in your flower garden or in your neighbour's garden.

Wait until they come out to collect the newspaper and see astonishment.

Then you can tell them that they are April Fools.

COFFEE HAS RUINED THE COMPUTER!

Coffee is the last thing that anybody wants spilled on their computer.

It can ruin it.

You can buy fake spilled coffee in a joke shop or you can make it yourself if you have time and patience.

Choose a cup; preferably one that the target uses to drink his coffee.

Then mix together equal parts of white glue and brown puff paint until the colour is darker than the colour of coffee as it will fade a little as it dries.

Pour a teaspoon of the mixture onto greaseproof paper, set the tipped over cup into it and then add more liquid in front of the mug's lip.

Allow to dry. It may take up to a week.

When it is dry, gently peel back the greaseproof paper.

You now have your prop.

Just wait for the right time to set in place over the computer keyboard.

Watch the shit hit the fan.

MONEY FOR NOTHING

An oldie but a goody is to superglue some coins to the sidewalk or any spot that has a lot of people walking around.

Watch while people try to pick them up.

WHAT A MESS!

Cut out the bottom of a shoebox and glue on the lid. Fill the cavity with peanut shells or some other light material and place the box on a colleague's desk so that it looks intact.

The victim will pick up the mysterious box and send the contents all over the place.

TIME WASTER

Try sending one of your colleagues on a pointless errand.

A BAD CASE OF DANDRUFF

Pour salt in your hair and then complain and scratch your head saying that it is itching badly.

Watch and be amused as workmates, spotting the scaly-looking white stuff cascading all over the place, gingerly keep out of your way while all the time trying not to offend you.

NOW WHERE IS IT?

This is best played on someone in the family.

Sew up the fly on a clean pair of the target's underwear.

Make sure the victim drinks plenty of morning juice and coffee or tea and wait.

The most challenging part is ensuring that Dad selects the doctored pair on April Fool's morning.

APRIL FOOL'S DAY JOKE—WITHOUT DOING ANYTHING!

In the last couple of weeks in March, warn your friend several times in conversation that this year you have the best April Fool's joke ever.

Act in an excited way about 1 April approaching by saying things like, 'Only two days to the best day of the year!'

On the morning of April Fool's Day, act excitedly and repeatedly ask your friend how he/she is feeling, is he/she worried, does he/she have a sense of foreboding?

Keep looking at your watch and mumbling things like, 'Not long to go now.'

At midday, when April Fool's Day officially ends, your friend will finally breathe a big sigh of relief because he/she hasn't been a victim of a practical joke.

At least that's what he/she thinks.

The fact that you didn't play a practical joke was a joke in itself because you had them so worried.

Explain that the joke was the fact you didn't play a joke.

FAMILY FUN FOR APRIL FOOL'S DAY

Little brothers or sisters are very easy targets on April Fool's Day. They are so uncomplicated and gullible, that they will believe almost anything that a trusted person tells them.

Be gentle and don't break their trust, but make it a fun day for them.

WHAT'S THAT ON THE FRONT LAWN?

Stand at the window and exclaim that the stork has just dropped another baby on your front lawn.

Little brother/sister will come running over to see a Cabbage Patch doll all wrapped up and lying in the grass.

When he/she races outside to pick it up say, 'April Fool.'

DELICIOUS POO

Scatter some chocolate bullets around the floor.

When little brother/sister is watching exclaim, 'Oh that filthy cat! It has been pooing on the floor again.'

Pick one or two up, smell it and then put it in your mouth. Say, 'Yep, cat's poo.'

Get the broom and sweep the rest up.

Walk out of the room and watch the kid's mouth open.

SPOILING FOR A FIGHT

Let your teenage sister see you with her favourite top in one hand and a pair of scissors in the other.

When she can hear you, talk to your Mum saying that this is the perfect fabric for the school project you are doing designing doll's clothes.

Watch her go red in the face.

APRIL COLOUR

For a harmless April Fool's joke, add a few drops of food colouring to your milk if it comes in a cardboard container.

It is a colourful way to start the day.

WHERE AM I?

On the night before April Fool's Day, quietly shift the children from their own beds and to put them in another family member's bed.

Watch and laugh as they awake to April Fool's Day in another room—and in utter confusion.

FOOLED ON THE AIR WAVES

Over the years, newspapers, magazines and TV and radio stations have loved April Fool's Day.

They put out 'news' stories that sound believable—although a bit odd—and sit back and watch the fun.

One of the most celebrated was the TV report on 'The Spaghetti Tree'.

It was done in the UK in 1957 and a few years later in Melbourne, Australia. It showed the reporter standing in front of a tree, which had strands of cooked spaghetti hanging all over it! The reporter went on about how climactic and other conditions had caused the trees not to produce so much spaghetti that year, causing a downturn in the crop and having an impact on the worldwide economy. It was very convincingly done and a lot of people believed him.

'Those poor spaghetti farmers,' people were heard to say.

Many people were also taken in by a national Australian magazine, which presented the view of a Professor who announced that our concept of time would be changed.

Instead of 60 seconds in a minute, 60 minutes in an hour, 24 hours in a day and so on, we would have Decimal Time, with 100 seconds in a minute, 100 minutes in an hour and so on.

He had all the calculations, plus new names for the 10 months of the year.

'Decimal Time, based on 10, will be much easier for everyone to understand,' he declared.

Accompanying it was a photo of an academic looking man, holding a clock bearing only 10 figures, instead of the usual twelve.

A lot of people started to believe it, until closer scrutiny showed that the new system would start on April 1 and that the academic looked suspiciously like one of the magazine's well-known reporters dressed up in coke-bottle glasses and white coat.

The clincher was that he called himself 'Professor Fulsdeigh . . .'

On April Fool's Day in 2004, a Melbourne radio show announced that they had received an old tape from a lady who had been cleaning out her attic and that on it was a song, apparently recorded 50 or 60 years ago, which sounded very much like the Kylie Minogue hit, 'Can't Get You Out of My Head'.

It was a male voice, sung in the tenor voice popular at the time, with crackles and pops indicating its age.

Wow! Had the song—a hit for Kylie as well as being a big selling album track—been plagiarised by the two writers who claimed to have written it?

The announcer rang the publisher of the song and discussed the millions of dollars worldwide that it had made and how due credit had not been given to the real lyricist.

TV stations endeavoured to follow the story up for the nightly news and the daily paper also wasted valuable resources on follow up.

It was an April Fool's gag. The radio host, a former musician with a rock band, had sung and recorded the version of the song in his home studio, adding the crackles and pops to give it authenticity.

BABY PHOTOS

Everyone has photos of themselves as babies.

Most people do not want these photos seen by their friends.

If you can get your hands on a colleague's baby photos, you can cause a lot of embarrassment.

This is what you do:

- Get hold of one of the victim's baby photos.
- Scan the photo into a computer and print out lots of copies. Or, make photocopies of it.
- Get to work early one morning, long before the victim turns up.
- Stick the photos up all over the office, with a little sign saying, 'Frank, taken just before he started working here.'
- Also, you can do all sorts of things once you have the photo. There are many other places where you can stick up baby photos of your victim.
- You can make a Wanted sign and post it up in the neighbourhood.
- You can send it as an attachment to the corporate mailing list. If you really want to ensure that you will get fired, put a caption underneath, saying: 'A fine example of the amazing talent of our company.'

- You can add some smart comments and post it in places your boss frequents.
- You can place it over a bar with a notice saying, 'Don't serve this man.'

TECHNOLOGY JOKES

If you are good with computers the sky is the limit to the fun you can have!

But be careful to stay within the law.

DISABLED ICONS

Take a screen shot of your friend's computer's desktop.

Then open a graphics program and select 'Paste'.

This will create an image of the victim's desktop.

Save this file into the c:\windows\directory as a bitmap (bmp) and set it as the desktop background.

Then simply remove the icons from the desktop (either place them in a folder or, on some machines, you can select 'hide all desktop content').

When they sit down at their computer none of the icons will work.

SPECIAL DAYS

It is possible to design a point-of-sale system which, when activated, will react and cause great hilarity.

WE WISH YOU A MERRY CHRISTMAS, WE ...

For example, you could design a program that flashes lights and sounds beepers and wishes all the computers on the network at a given time and date, greetings of some kind or another.

Valentine's Day, New Year, Christmas or Easter are good times to select.

FOOTBALL

A program could be devised so that on a Friday in the football season, your team's theme song flashes throughout the network as the colours flash.

Or, if your team is playing a friend's team and your team wins, design a program so that when he switches on, on Monday morning, your team's theme lights up on his computer, loud and clear!

PAGERS

S end messages to pagers that say 'Low Battery'.

WHERE DID THAT COME FROM?

A lter the settings in Microsoft AutoCorrect so that whenever your victim types a specific word, for example their name, it is replaced with something more comical—a nickname for example or a nicely decorative name like 'Barge-arse' or 'Dickless'.

RING A DING

U sing sticky-tape, tape down the rocker on someone's phone so that when it is lifted it keeps on ringing.

This is really funny when your friends start saying 'Hello can I help you . . . er . . . eh?'

BIRTHDAY MESSAGE

Y ou could program in the birthdays of staff members and on that day have a birthday message flash on the screen every two hours.

GAME ENDS

If you have the sort of job where colleagues are hooked on a particular computer game, i.e. Tetris or Monopoly, there is ample opportunity to just tweak the program so that on a given signal the game ends abruptly, just when they are about to achieve a milestone and a fireworks display takes over.

UNTAMED MOUSEY

Click the start button and then go to Settings—Control Panel. Open Mouse and change the button configuration to left handed (assuming it was originally at right handed).

Then put the mouse speed up to the maximum.

The mouse will be really hard to use!

FOR TOUCH TYPISTS

For the person who can touch type really well, remove all the keys from their keyboard (carefully!) and put them back in alphabetic order.

You will be surprised just how slow their typing suddenly becomes!

Instead of changing the whole keyboard, only switch the 'm' and the 'n' keys. This works best for people who can touch type well.

RELUCTANT MOUSE

Stick a Post-it note under your friend's mouse so that the paper leaf covers the mouse ball—the mouse will no longer work!

Align so that the sticky part of the note doesn't touch the ball.

Costs next to nothing to do and doesn't cause any damage.

MODEM MAYHEM

If your colleague's computer relies on a modem it can be very funny to change the telephone number that their computer dials up when connecting to the internet to that of their mobile phone!

Every time they try to connect their mobile will ring and when they answer it they'll just hear strange noises.

NB: You must write down and keep the original phone number so that you can put the real number back to what it should be.

FREE PROGRAMS THAT CAN BE USED FOR PRANKS

The internet offers free-to-user sites where you can download programs that will mystify and frustrate your colleagues.

Here are a few examples from www.thefreesite.com.

There is a free program that will cause your victim's screen to go black or capture the desktop and display as a bitmap image. The victim of your prank will then be unable to close the screen without a password. Black Screen can be used as a joke gag or for security purposes.

Mystify your computer friends with a program which inexplicably opens the CD drive. You can change a shortcut on a commonly used application to point to this gag program, sit back and let the fun begin as they try to figure out what the heck's going on!

A joke program simulates the Windows program crash dialog box. And it's difficult to tell that it's a fake! It's easy to use and there is no setup/install involved. Just copy the program to someone's machine and run it.

Another free gag program allows you to set up a message dialog to be displayed on someone's computer. You can specify the text to be displayed, as well as the type of message box. You can also specify when the message will be displayed, among other options.

If you're a Webmaster and you'd like to play a practical joke on your visitors, then check out the free JavaScript that offers a scary pop-up message that tells visitors they have a computer virus.

An exceedingly cruel, free prank program simulates the deletion of all files and folders in your victim's Windows directory. Looks very real and even experienced users will be unable to detect or stop it. You can select the directory to be deleted. This new version even features the added realism of hard drive noise!

Install the free joke program that displays a button on the desktop. When your prank victim moves their mouse to click on the button, it moves elsewhere! Lots of fun.

A free utility will toggle the Num Lock or Scroll Lock keys at intervals that you can specify. You can set up which keys to toggle and how often they'll be toggled. New version includes command line support for Num, Caps and Scroll Lock.

Launch another of the free programs on your unsuspecting victim and watch their reaction when the Windows cursor changes to a rude gesture that involves the middle finger! By default, this program will switch the standard cursor to a finger every five seconds, but you can configure how often the cursor will change.

A sneaky gag program offers all kinds of possibilities for driving your colleagues bananas. It's a hidden program launcher that'll execute a specified program or .wav file at intervals that you choose. You can specify when the program or sound file will be launched, as well as how often it'll be launched. Fun!

THERE'S MORE!

Here's a collection of funny alternative free splash screens for your Windows machine. Various gags are here.

There is a free utility that randomly switches your Windows desktop wallpaper at any interval that you select. It's a stealth program (meaning that it can't be detected). Good either as a prank or if you'd just like to have a new wallpaper automatically displayed, from time to time.

Drive your friends insane with the prank program Fake Format.

When executed, it gives the appearance that your hard drive is being formatted. Your victim will be unable to stop or close this clever, realistic program. It even creates hard drive noise while it is formatting.

A nifty, free prank program makes it realistically appear as though an unwanted file is being downloaded from the Net. DownHoax randomly chooses a site from its internal database of undesirables and proceeds to simulate downloading an equally distasteful file. Supports both Netscape and Internet Explorer.

Another program simulates a realistic-looking Windows crash screen gag that won't go away, but causes no harm to the computer.

Randomly change the appearance of the mouse cursor. It allows you to choose which cursor to change, what type of cursor to change it to and how often you'd like to swap the cursor. Cursor Fun is great for playing a trick on an unsuspecting user or for those who get bored easily with their desktop.

Rude noises for your listening pleasure. Install the Fart Machine, open the program from your start menu and simply double click on the rude sound that you want to hear. From the wacky guys at Wavhounds.com.

WILD GOOSE CHASES

Direct your colleague to a web address that you create. Make up news items about him/her and including his/her name.

Send your colleague to a website that you have created with the most amazing but untrue fact. Make sure that they are not too unbelievable or else he/she won't be interested.

A website named www.StrangeReports.com has sites that are already compiled for this purpose.

This site has forms and websites for the following:
- overdue books
- nose pickers society
- police warrants
- toilet paper thief
- hacker news
- jock strap thief
- cigarette butt thief.

BEHAVING ERRATICALLY

This works especially well on older people or people who:
1. Are new to computers; or
2. Rely heavily on the keypad at the right of the keyboard.

Simply press the numlock key when they aren't looking.

They will wonder why the 'number keys' just move the cursor around!

BLACK ON BLACK

Change the prompt on someone's computer to be black on black. This is rather cruel if the person is computer illiterate.

Very effective the day before a big project is due.

SOUNDS SIMPLE

It is possible to play sounds remotely on some workstations. You can have all kinds of fun playing sounds like flushing toilets and other unusual sounds.

Works best if the person is relatively new to the job.

DOORS JAMMED

Superglue the drive doors shut as well as all the relevant power switches in the 'on' position and the power cables to the wall.

DOTS

Write a small program that prints 'Formatting C:' and starts printing a series of dots at intervals afterwards.

Simulate disk access by continuously creating and deleting an empty text file.

Write a command that sends each individual page of a print job to a different printer on the network. Select the printer at random.

Put an intercom inside a machine and then convince some nerd that it is an AI with voice recognition.

Convince a new person that there has been a virus going around that presents hypnotic patterns on the screen which can really mess up your mind.

Then start up remotely or set to start at a particular time a fractal program of some sort.

They'll probably panic big time.

Write a TSR that turns the keyboard on and off at short intervals.

You'll watch the person try keyboard after keyboard.

Can also swap keys using ANSI.SYS or xmodemap depending on the system.

Convert a XXX image to a bitmap and make it someone's OS/2 or Windows background.

Change the background of someone's X-Windows session remotely as well as make a picture appear. They can't stop you.

Rig the spring in a Macintosh floppy drive to fire the disk a goodly distance from the machine upon ejection.

Reverse the turbo switch so that the machine runs fast when it should run slow and slow when it should be fast.

If they haven't changed the default password for their BIOS, change it yourself and lock them out of their machine.

Write fake disaster error messages that appear at random time.

CABLE PROBLEMS

When someone is watching TV and leaves the room for a minute, change to a channel that your TV doesn't pick up, so it's all fuzzy and then you leave the room.

When your target comes back he'll think the cable is messed up.

Enjoy watching as they search for the problem.

I WISH I'D SAID THAT!

Conversation stoppers

Pop these into the conversation at the appropriate times—and wait for the response, which could be a laugh, puzzlement or anger.

- I drive way too fast to worry about cholesterol.
- Laughing stock? They're cattle with a sense of humour, aren't they?
- Depression is merely anger without enthusiasm.
- I almost had a psychic girlfriend, but she left me before we met.
- If you ain't making waves, you ain't kicking hard enough!
- Support bacteria—they're the only culture some people have.
- The only substitute for good manners is fast reflexes.
- When everything's coming your way, you're in the wrong lane.
- Ambition is a poor excuse for not having enough sense to be lazy.
- Beauty is in the eye of the beer holder.
- If everything seems to be going well, you have obviously overlooked something.
- Everyone has a photographic memory. Some just don't have the film.
- I poured Spot remover on my dog. Now he's gone.
- I couldn't repair your brakes, so I made your horn louder.

- Shin: a device for finding furniture in the dark.
- How do you tell when you run out of invisible ink?
- Join the Army, meet interesting people and kill them.
- Why do psychics have to ask you for your name?
- Wear short sleeves! Support your right to bare arms.
- Corduroy pillows: They're making headlines!
- Black holes are where God divided by zero.
- I tried sniffing Coke once, but the ice cubes got stuck in my nose.

PICK UP NO-NOS

Here are some pick up lines to give your young brother to make sure that he remains a virgin for life.

- I wish you were a door so I could bang you all day long.
- Nice legs. What time do they open?
- Do you work for the post office? I thought I saw you checking out my package.
- You have 206 bones in your body, want one more?
- I'm a bird watcher and I'm looking for a Big Breasted Bed Thrasher. Have you seen one?
- I'm fighting the urge to make you the happiest woman on earth tonight.
- I'd really like to see how you look when I'm naked.
- You must be the limp doctor, because I've got a stiffy.
- You know, if I were you, I'd have sex with me.
- You, me, whipped cream and handcuffs. Any questions?
- Those clothes would look great in a crumpled heap on my bedroom floor.
- Hi, the voices in my head told me to come over and talk to you.
- (Lick finger and wipe on her shirt.) 'Let's get you out of those wet clothes.'
- You know what would look good on you? Me . . .

TEN RULES FOR DIETING

Post these on the refrigerator, to keep your flatmates amused and confused.

1. I might be a fat bastard, but at least I'm a happy fat bastard.
2. If you eat something and no one else sees you eat it, it has no calories and therefore does not count.
3. When drinking a diet soda while eating a candy bar, the calories in the candy bar are automatically cancelled by the diet soda.
4. When you eat with someone else, calories don't count as long as you don't eat more than they do.
5. You can always move up a size in clothes and not tell anyone.
6. Foods used for medicinal purposes never count. Example: hot chocolate, brandy, toast, cheesecake.
7. If you fatten up everyone else around you, then you look thinner.
8. If you are in the process of preparing something, any food licked off knives and spoons has no calories.
9. Any clear spirit, such as vodka or gin, is obviously the same as water and has no calories.
10. Have you ever known a thin person who actually enjoys life?

BOURKE'S LAWS:

- The success of any venture will be helped by prayer, even in the wrong Denomination.
- When things are going well, someone will inevitably experiment detrimentally.
- The deficiency will never show itself during the dry runs.

- Information travels more surely to those with a lesser need to know.
- An original idea can never emerge from a committee.
- When the product is destined to fail, the delivery system will perform perfectly.
- The lagging activity in a project will invariably be found in the area where the highest overtime rates lie waiting.
- The 'think positive' leader tends to listen to his subordinates' premonitions only during the post-mortems.
- Clearly stated instructions will consistently produce multiple interpretations.

OXYMORONS

- act naturally
- happily married
- Microsoft works
- holy war
- found missing
- resident alien
- advanced basic
- genuine imitation
- airline food
- good grief
- government organization
- everything except
- civil war
- sanitary landfill
- alone together
- legally drunk
- silent scream
- British fashion
- living dead

- small crowd
- business ethics
- soft rock
- butt head
- military intelligence
- software documentation
- New York culture
- new classic
- sweet sorrow
- childproof
- 'now, then'
- synthetic natural gas
- Christian scientists
- passive aggressive
- taped live
- clearly misunderstood
- peace force
- extinct life
- temporary tax increase
- computer jock
- plastic glasses
- terribly pleased
- computer security
- political science
- tight slacks
- definite maybe
- pretty ugly
- twelve-ounce pound cake
- diet ice cream
- rap music
- working vacation
- exact estimate
- religious tolerance
- freezer burn

- honest politician
- jumbo shrimp
- loners club
- postal service.

CONDOM PROMOTION

Paste one of these on your mate's condom packet:

- Cover your stump before you hump.
- Don't be silly, protect your willy.
- When in doubt, shroud your spout.
- Don't be a loner, cover your boner.
- You can't go wrong if you shield your dong.
- If you think she's spunky, cover your monkey.
- If you slip between her thighs, be sure to condomize.
- If you go into heat, package your meat.
- Especially in December, gift wrap your member.
- Don't be a fool, vulcanise your tool.
- The right selection! Protect your erection.
- Wrap it in foil before checking her oil.
- If you really love her, wear a cover.
- Don't make a mistake! Muzzle your snake.
- Never deck her with an unwrapped pecker.
- If you can't shield your rocket, leave it in your pocket.
- No glove, No love.
- Don't be in such a jiffy, cover your stiffy.
- AIDS is no joke, be sure to wrap before you poke.

DON'T GET ANGRY, GET EVEN

Every now and then, life presents a little challenge, which cannot go unanswered, Here's a practical guide to getting back at someone when you reckon you have been wronged.

SUFFER, LOVER!

This is a safe and fool proof way to make the life of a lover who has treated you badly miserable for a few weeks.

Make up flyers with his picture and phone number stating something like, 'Bisexual male looking for casual or long-term relationship'.

Post it all around the city, in supermarkets, coffee shops and even a gay dance club.

The constant phone calls will be distressing for both him and his new lover.

Serve him right.

STORY TOLD

Write an article in your local newspaper, the company newsletter or just a circular that you send out yourself.

Spell out the whole story of the dirty rotten sod's misadventures so that the whole community is warned against him/her.

MISSING SOMETHING?

Wait until he/she goes to sleep and sneak into his/her room and shave one eyebrow off.

Pretend to know nothing about it.

Enjoy his/her discomfort.

IN IT TOGETHER

If you have a teacher who is a total bastard make him pay.

If there is even only one student at school, it is the teacher's duty of care to be there with them.

Stay behind, on the pretence that you have some work to do.

Make him suffer.

He will have to supervise you.

FALSE ALARM

Have you a 'friend' who has been fooling around and pretends to be worried that she may be pregnant?

Here's a way to make her think more carefully.

Buy her a home pregnancy test.

Enlist the aid of a friend who is in early pregnancy.

Get the girl who did the dirty on you to go to your bathroom and do the pregnancy test.

Get your pregnant friend in to do the test, unknown to the dirty rotten double crossing 'friend', switch the result and she will think that it is her result and will be very worried.

MINE IS BIGGER THAN YOURS

Do you know somebody who is always bragging and who always goes one better than everyone else?

Ply him with copious amounts of drink.

When he has had so much that he can hardly stand up, be a good angel and take him to his room.

Lay him on his bed where he will sleep like a baby.

Now he is yours to play any prank.

Shave half his moustache; shave one eyebrow; shave any hairs around one man-boob.

Let him wake up next day feeling like death and wondering what happened to him.

WRAPPED CAR

Have a double-timer on your hands? On a hot day take a large roll of plastic wrap, which people use to cover leftovers, and go out when nobody can see you.

You wrap the double timing sod's car in the stuff.

Next day, when it heats up, just watch it melt and become really hard to take off!

HYGIENE

If the dirty double crossing rat leaves his/her toothbrush around, simply dip it in the toilet, clean the bath with it or poke it up your nose.

Replace it in the holder.

You will find the right time to let them know.

OH NO!

Most guys love their car.

If you have been treated badly, get him where it hurts most, in the car!

Buy 500 condoms from the supermarket.

Crazy glue them all over the car.

When he tries to pull them off he will be left with all the little rings from the end of the condoms.

SPLASH!

Fill a glass with water.

It is important that you use a glass and not a plastic or paper cup.

Tell the victim that you are going to nail the glass of water to a wall. The victim will not believe you can succeed and will be keen to watch you fail.

Ask the victim to hold the hammer for you. (This gets them used to helping you.)

Place the glass against the wall.

Begin to put the nail in place, then drop the nail to the floor beneath the glass.

Ask the victim to pick the nail up for you because you cannot let go of the glass.

When the victim is under the glass, tip the glass upside down so that the water falls onto their head.

EMAIL LISTS

Here's some stuff that makes sense actually—and which you can send around.

- Better to be safe than punch a 5th grader.
- Strike while the bug is close.
- It's always darkest before daylight savings time.
- Don't bite the hand that . . . looks dirty.
- No news is impossible.
- A miss is as good as a Mr.
- You can't teach an old dog new maths.
- If you lie down with dogs, you will stink in the morning.
- Love all, trust . . . me.
- An idle mind is the best way to relax.
- Where there is smoke, there's . . . pollution.
- Happy is the bride who gets all the presents.
- A penny saved is not much.
- Two is company, three's The Musketeers.
- None are so blind as Helen Keller.
- Children should be seen and not spanked or grounded.
- If at first you don't succeed get new batteries.
- When the blind lead the blind . . . get out of the way.
- Laugh and the whole world laughs with you. Cry and you have to blow your nose.

UNREAL ESTATE

If you know anybody who is in the market, looking to buy a house, send this list to them so that they are aware of 'realestatespeak' and what it exactly means.

The joke will be on the real estate agent, because your friend won't be beaten by all the jargon.

Charming   Tiny.

Much potential   All of it undeveloped and guaranteed to cause nervous breakdown.

Unique city home   Was a factory; walls are concrete and cold; smells of grease.

Daring design   Still a warehouse.

Contemporary   Cheaply constructed in a hurry to the advantage of 'first home buyers grant'.

Completely updated   Stainless steel appliances, floorboards, courtyard instead of a garden.

Sophisticated   Black walls and no windows.

One-of-a-kind   Ugly as sin. Nothing quite like it still standing.

Brilliant concept   Do you really need a two storey live oak in your 30 foot sky dome?

You'll love it   No, you won't.

Must see to believe   Unless you saw it, you'd never believe it.

Renovator's delight   A dump.

Garden outlook   You get a good view of the neighbour's garden.

Sea glimpses   Stand on your toes, on the seat of the dunny, in the laundry toilet and you may see some blue.

A MEDICAL DICTIONARY

Had anything to do with the medical fraternity lately? Or if you know somebody who has, then send them this one.
You'll all feel a lot better for it.

Artery	The study of painting.
Bacteria	The back door of the cafeteria.
Barium	What the doctors do when patients die.
Caesarean section	A neighbourhood in Rome.
Cat scan	Searching for a kitty.
Cauterize	Made eye contact with her.
Colic	A sheep dog.
Dilate	To live long.
Enema	Not a friend.
Fester	Quicker.
GI series	A Soldiers Ball Game.
Impotent	Distinguished, well known.
Labour pain	Getting hurt at work.
Medical staff	A doctor's cane.
Morbid	A higher offer.
Nitrates	Cheaper than day rates.
Node	Was aware of.
Pap smear	A fatherhood test.
Pelvis	A cousin to Elvis.
Post operative	A letter carrier.
Recovery room	A place to do re-upholstery.
Rectum	Dang near killed 'em.
Seizure	A Roman Emperor.
Tablet	A small table.
Terminal illness	Getting sick at the airport.
Tumour	More than one.
Urine	Opposite of you're out.
Varicose	Nearby.

IT'S GOING TO BE A ROTTEN DAY IF . . .

1. You wake face down on the footpath.
2. You put your bra on backwards and it fits better.
3. You call Suicide Prevention and they put you on hold.

4. You see a '60 Minutes' team waiting in your office.
5. Your birthday cake collapses from the weight of the candles.
6. You want to put on clothes you wore home from the party and there aren't any.
7. You put on the news and they're showing emergency routes out of the city.
8. Your twin forgot your birthday.
9. The car horn goes off accidentally and remains stuck while you're following a group of Hell's Angels.
10. The boss tells you not to bother taking off your coat.
11. The bird singing outside your window is a vulture.
12. You walk to work and then find your dress is stuck in the back of your pantyhose (even more embarrassing if you're not a woman!).
13. You call your answering service and they tell you it's none of your business.
14. Your blind date turns out to be your wife.
15. Your income tax cheque bounces.
16. You put both contact lenses in the same eye.
17. Your wife says 'Good morning Bill' and your name is Frank!

THINGS TO PONDER

- Why is it when you open a can of evaporated milk it's still full?
- Why do shops which are open 24/7 have locks on the doors?
- If quitters never win and winners never quit, what fool came up with, 'Quit while you're ahead'?
- Women should put pictures of missing husbands on beer cans.
- Employment application blanks always ask who is to be notified in case of an emergency. I think you should write . . . a good doctor.
- Before they invented drawing boards, what did they go back to?
- Is it possible to have a civil war?
- If all the world is a stage, where does the audience sit?
- If you ate pasta and antipasto, would you still be hungry?
- If you try to fail and succeed, which have you done?

- Is a castrated pig disgruntled?
- Why is it called tourist season if we can't shoot at them?
- Why is the alphabet in that order? Is it because of that song?
- If the black box flight recorder is never damaged during a plane crash, why isn't the whole airplane made out of the stuff?
- Why is there an expiration date on sour cream?
- If most car accidents occur within five miles of home, why doesn't everyone just move ten miles away?
- Light travels faster than sound so is that why some people appear bright until you hear them speak?
- Does the reverse side also have a reverse side?
- Why is a carrot more orange than an orange?
- Why are there five syllables in the word 'monosyllabic'?
- Why is it that when a door is open, it's ajar, but when a jar is open, it's not a door?
- How much deeper would the ocean be, if sponges didn't grow in it?
- If all those psychics know the winning lottery numbers, why are they all still working?
- Why is abbreviated such a long word?
- Why is there only one Monopolies Commission?
- Is the leaning Tower of Pisa a listed building?
- What if there were no hypothetical questions?

WHAT DO LABELS REALLY MEAN?

Labels—proof that the world is going crazy:

On Sears hairdryer.
(Do not use while sleeping.)

On a bag of Fritos.
(You could be a winner! No purchase necessary. Details inside.)

On a bar of Dial soap.
(Directions: Use like regular soap.)

On some Swann frozen dinners.
(Serving suggestion: Defrost.)

On a hotel provided shower cap in a box.
(Fits one head.)

On Tesco's Tiramisu dessert.
([Printed on bottom of the box.] Do not turn upside down.)

On Marks & Spencer Bread Pudding.
(Product will be hot after heating.)

On packaging for an iron.
(Do not iron clothes on body.)

On Boot's Children's cough medicine.
(Do not drive car or operate machinery.)

On sleep aid.
(Warning: may cause drowsiness.)

On a Korean kitchen knife.
(Warning keep out of children.)

On a string of Chinese-made Christmas lights.
(For indoor or outdoor use only.)

On a Japanese food processor.
(Not to be used for the other use.)

On Sainsbury's peanuts.
(Warning: contains nuts.)

On an American Airlines packet of nuts.
(Instructions: open packet, eat nuts.)

On a Swedish chain saw.
(Do not attempt to stop chain with your hands or genitals.)

On a child's superman costume.
(Wearing of this garment does not enable you to fly.)

BOOKS WHICH HAVE NO CONTENT

- The Code of Ethics for Lawyers
- The Australian Book of Foreplay
- The Book of Motivated Postal Workers
- Americans' Guide to Etiquette
- Royal Family's Guide to Good Marriages
- Cultured Places to Travel in the USA
- Bill Clinton: A Portrait of Integrity
- George Bush: Man of Peace
- Contraception, by Pope John Paul II
- Cooking Gourmet Dishes With Tofu
- The Complete Guide to Catholic Sex
- The Wit and Wisdom of Dan Quayle
- Consumer Marketing Ethics
- John Howard: The Wild Years
- Popular Lawyers
- Career Opportunities for History Majors
- Everything Men Know about Women
- Great Women Drivers of Today
- Home Built Airplanes, by John Denver
- Things I Love About Bill, by Hillary Clinton

- My Life's Memories, by Ronald Reagan
- Things I Can't Afford, by Bill Gates

YOU ARE A CHILD OF THE '80S, IF:

- You had a crush on one of the New Kids on the Block members.
- You wanted to be on *Star Search*.
- You can remember what Michael Jackson looked like before his nose fell off.
- You wore a banana clip or one of those slap on wrist bands at some point during your youth.
- You had slouch socks and puff painted your own shirt at least once.
- You know the profound meaning of 'Wax on, Wax off'.
- You can name at least half of the members of the elite 'Brat Pack'.
- You can recite the whole script for both *Grease* and *Saturday Night Fever.*
- You have seen at least 10 episodes of *Fraggle Rock*.
- You know that another name for a keyboard is a 'Synthesiser'.
- You hold a special place in your heart for *Back to the Future*.
- You know what 'Sike' means.
- You fell victim to '80's fashion: big hair, crimped, combed over to the side and you wore spandex pants.
- You owned an extensive collection of Cabbage Patch Kids and trolls.
- You wore fluorescent—clothing or nail polish.
- You could break dance or wished you could.
- You remember when Atari was a state of the art video game system.
- You own any cassettes.
- You were led to believe that in the year 2000 we'd all be living on the Moon.
- You remember and/or own any of the Care Bear Glass collection from Pizza Hut.
- *Poltergeist*, the movie, freaked you out.
- You carried your lunch to school in a Gremlins or an ET lunchbox.

- You pondered why Smurfette was the only female Smurf.
- You wanted to have an alien like Alf living in your house.
- You wore biker shorts underneath a short skirt and felt stylish.
- You wore tights under shorts and felt stylish.
- You had a Swatch Watch.
- You spent countless hours trying to perfect the Care-Bear stare.
- You remember when *Saturday Night Live* was funny.
- You had Wonder Woman or Superman underwear.
- You thought that Transformers were more than meets the eye.
- Partying 'like it's 1999' seemed so far away!

MASHED TATORS AND OTHERS

Some people never seem motivated to participate, but are content to watch others do . . . They are called 'Speck Tators'.

Some people never do anything to help, but are gifted at finding fault with the way others do things . . . They're called 'Comment Tators'.

Some are always looking to cause problems and really get under your skin . . . They are called 'Aggie Tators'.

There are those who are always saying they will, but somehow, they never get around to doing . . . We call them 'Hezzie Tators'.

Some people put on a front and act like someone else . . . They're called 'Emma Tators'.

Then, there are those who walk what they talk. They're always prepared to stop what they're doing to lend a hand to others and bring real sunshine into the lives of others. You can call them 'Sweet Tators'.

CONFUCIUS SAY:

- War doesn't determine who is right, war determines who is left.
- Man with one chopstick go hungry.
- Man with hand in pocket feel cocky all day.
- Virginity like bubble, one prick all gone.
- Passionate kiss like spider's web, soon lead to undoing of fly.
- Man who run in front of car get tired.
- Man who run behind car get exhausted.
- Crowded elevator smells different to midget.
- Man who fishes in other man's well often catches crabs.
- Man who scratches ass should not bite fingernails.
- Man who eat many prunes get good run for money.
- Man who fight with wife all day get no piece at night.
- It take many nails to build crib but one screw to fill it.
- Man who drive like hell bound to get there.
- Man who stand on toilet is high on pot.

YOU AND YOUR STARS

Aries

You tend to be headstrong and deliberate in your actions. Basically you don't give a shit about anyone. Most people hate you but you couldn't care less. You're the type of person who would masturbate at a wedding.

Taurus

Warm and caring are your most endearing characteristics. You get on well with most people because you're bisexual. You hardly ever wear underwear and you constantly smell of piss.

Gemini

Your star sign denotes an air of duality in your character. Simply, you're a neurotic schizophrenic. A real bloody weirdo, the type of person who'd kill yourself to win a bet.

Cancer

You have a businesslike attitude to life and a knack for making money. You're an unscrupulous bastard who would sell a relative's limbs to buy a mobile phone. You are likely to be murdered.

Leo

The adventurous type, always looking for thrills and willing to try anything. In other words, stupid. You have the IQ of a garden snail and will never amount to anything. Most Leos are living on the welfare.

Virgo

You like the good things in life and you know how to enjoy them. But you're prone to bullshitting and you're a cheap bastard. Virgo men are usually queers and the majority of Virgo women are whores.

Libra

You are the forgiving type and you don't bear grudges. This makes you an asshole. For your entire life people will make a complete prick out of you. Nobody will go to your funeral.

Scorpio

You are sharp, a quick thinker and good at puzzles. However these are your only good traits. You screw small animals and love picking your nose. You should become a stunt performer with no helmet.

Sagittarius

You are the romantic mushy type, soft-hearted and a lover of the arts. You are likely to import Dutch pornography and sex toys. Men willing to rent *Sleepless In Seattle* can increase your odds for a romp in the sack.

Capricorn

You are deep and personal in your thoughts, the quiet type. A mean self-centred prick and a closet homosexual. Your best friend is probably an altar boy.

Aquarius

You are the academic type and will probably end up working in the legal system. This means you are an absolute pervert, at the least a transvestite. Your ideal sexual partner is a Labrador puppy wearing fishnet tights.

Pisces

You are the eternal optimist, seeing the best of any situation. You have no grasp of reality and live in a dream world. Most people consider you to be the greatest living moron. You will continually fail. You're a prick.

MEN ARE LIKE:

Placemats—	they only show up when there's food on the table.
Mascara—	they usually run at the first sign of emotion.
Bike helmets—	they're good in emergencies but usually just look silly.
Government bonds—	they take so long to mature.
Copiers—	you need them in reproduction, but that's about it.
Lava lamps—	fun to look at but not all that bright.

Bank accounts—	without a lot of money they don't generate a lot of interest.
High heels—	they're easy to walk on once you get the hang of it.
Curling irons—	they're always hot and always in your hair.
Mini skirts—	if you're not careful, they'll creep up your legs.
Handguns—	keep one around long enough and you're gonna want to shoot it.

RULES FOR MEN

The Female always makes The Rules.

The Rules are subject to change at any time without prior notification.

No Male can possibly know all The Rules.

If the Female suspects the Male knows all The Rules, she must immediately change some or all of The Rules.

The Female is never wrong.

If the Female is wrong, it is because of a flagrant misunderstanding which was a direct result of something the Male did or said wrong.

If the above Rule applies, the Male must apologise immediately for causing the misunderstanding.

The Female can change her mind at any given point in time.

The Male must never change his mind without express written consent from the Female.

The Female has every right to be angry or upset at any time.

The Male must remain calm at all times, unless the Female wants him to be angry or upset.

The Female must under no circumstances let the Male know whether or not she wants him to be angry or upset.

The Male is expected to mind read at all times.

The Male who doesn't abide by The Rules, can't take the heat, lacks a backbone and is a wimp.

Any attempt to document The Rules could result in bodily harm.

At no time can the Male make such comments as 'Insignificant', and 'Is that all?' when the Female is complaining.

If the Female has PMS, all The Rules are null and void . . .

WHICH CONDOM WOULD YOU USE?

Nike: Just do it.

Toyota: Oh, what a feeling.

Diet Pepsi: You got the right one, baby.

Pringles: Once you pop, you can't stop.

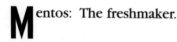

Mentos: The freshmaker.

Ford: The best never rest.

Yellow Pages: Aren't you glad you use it? Don't you wish everybody did?

Tatts Lotto: Who's next?

KFC: Finger-licking good.

Coca Cola: Always a real thing.

Campbell's Soup: Mm, mm good . . .

Mars Bar: The quicker picker upper.

Microsoft: Where do you want to go today?

Energizer: It keeps going and going and going . . .

M&Ms: 'It melts in your mouth, not in your hands!'

Taco Bell: Get some; make a run for the border.

Double Mint: Double your pleasure, double your fun!

United Airlines travel pack: Fly united.

The Star Trek Condom: To boldly go where no man has gone before.

Maxwell House: Good to the last drop!

Hewlett Packard: Expanding possibilities.

THE LIBRARY

The library is a great place for practical jokes. Here are some ways to have fun and to annoy other users.

- Read out loudly. Very loud. And slowly.
- While pointing to a very simple word, like 'the', ask the person next to you if he/she can pronounce it for you.
- While looking at your book, turn so you're facing the person. Then, peer over the top of your book and say 'PEEKABOO!'
- Look over your book and, in a most peculiar, psychotic way and say, 'You're one of THEM!'.
- Read your book. Upside down.
- Read your book from right to left. And flip the pages the same way.
- Flip the page every two or so seconds.
- Every so often, yelp in pain and look at your feet.
- Break the silence by making a bodily function noise, then say, 'Wow! That was a good one!'
- Every time the person next to you turns the page, make a strange sound or a beep.
- Announce the page number each time you turn a page.
- Sneeze a lot.
- Hold your book right next to your eyes.
- Every few minutes, get up out of your chair, walk around the table and sit back down.
- Bring a bottle of mouth freshener and miss every time you try to spray it into your mouth.
- Collapse on the floor. Then get up like nothing happened.

- Run up to them with a book, thrust it under their nose and ask, 'Will you sign my autograph?' Make sure you say 'my'.
- Glance over your shoulder every few seconds.
- Find a Thesaurus and say in complete astonishment, 'Wow! Did you know that "affirmative" and "yes" mean the same thing?'

LANGUAGE

The funniest practical jokes can be played without going to elaborate trouble to set things up. Just using our language—the written or spoken word—will do.

The jokes can be played in the course of your day at whatever business you happen to be in. Of course, some occupations allow more licence and scope to play word pranks on the gullible public.

The more subtle the joke, the more it will be enjoyed by a greater number of people. Remember to keep it believable and real.

Of all the professionals who have the greatest opportunity to play practical jokes on their public, the best placed people are Tour Guides and people who make their living by informing others.

Spinning a yarn is a great way to make the most of mundane days, interesting.

Playing out a running gag can be fun, but you must remember to keep it going until you get to the punch line.

PLAYS ON WORDS

Good morning. Before I began this job, I worked in an orange juice factory, but I got canned. I couldn't concentrate. My boss almost beat the pulp out of me. They really put the squeeze to me, too . . .

I used to work in a watch factory. I sat around making faces all day.

Here, take some advice. Never play leapfrog with a unicorn!

RUNNING GAGS

To be successful running gags must be played in sequence and over a period of time:

You know, a tiger can weigh over 500 pounds and leap up to 20 feet! Isn't that amazing!

And you know, a water buffalo can weigh over 500 pounds and leap up to 20 feet! Isn't that amazing!

Hey, guess what, did you know that a zebra can weigh over 500 pounds and leap up to 20 feet? Isn't that amazing!

And by the way, a snake can weigh up to 500 pounds and leap up to 20 feet! Isn't that amazing!

By the way, I hear you have a new girlfriend and she weighs over 500 pounds and can leap up to 20 feet!

OFFICE GUERRILLA

Don't let the bastards grind you down. Fight back in the workplace. At least when they fire you, you will know it has all been worth it.

TEN WAYS TO IRRITATE EVERYBODY AT YOUR WORKPLACE

1. Page yourself over the intercom. Don't disguise your voice.
2. Find out where your boss shops and buy exactly the same outfits. Wear them one day after you boss does. This is especially effective if your boss is of a different gender than you.
3. Make up nicknames for all your co-workers and refer to them only by these names. 'That's a good point, Sparky.' 'No, I'm sorry, but I'm going to have to disagree with you there, Cha-Cha.'
4. Put highlighter marks on your shoes. Tell people you haven't lost them as much since you did this.
5. Hang mosquito netting around your cubicle. When you emerge to get coffee or a printout or whatever, slap yourself randomly the whole way.
6. Put a chair facing a printer. Sit there all day and tell people you're waiting for your document.
7. Every time someone asks you to do something, anything, ask them if they want fries with that.
8. Encourage your colleagues to join you in a little synchronised chair-dancing.
9. Feign an unnatural and hysterical fear of staplers.
10. Send email messages saying there's free pizza in the lunchroom. When people drift back to work complaining that they found none, lean back, pat your stomach and say, 'Oh you've got to be quicker than that!'

NAPPING EXCUSES

Here are ten excellent excuses to use if someone comes up, hovers over your desk and catches you napping.

Train yourself so that when you suddenly wake up you automatically say one of these:

- '. . . in the name of the Lord Jesus, Amen.'
- 'Damn! Why did you interrupt me? I had almost figured out a solution to our biggest problem.'
- 'I was doing Yoga exercises to relieve work-related stress.'
- 'I was testing my keyboard for drool resistance.'
- 'I wasn't sleeping! I was meditating on the mission statement and envisioning a new paradigm.'
- 'Someone must've put decaf in the wrong pot . . .'
- 'The coffee machine is broken . . .'
- 'They told me at the blood bank this might happen.'
- 'This is just a 15 minute power-nap as described in that time management course you sent me.'
- 'Whew! Guess I left the top off the white-out. You probably got here just in time!'

OFFICE PRAYER

Whenever things get too much at the office, kneel by the side of your desk, bow your head and join your hands in prayer, saying loudly so that all can hear:

Grant me the serenity to accept the things I cannot change, the courage to change the things I cannot accept,

And the wisdom to hide the bodies of those people I had to kill today because they pissed me off.

Also, help me to be careful of the toes I step on today, as they may be connected to the ass I have to kiss tomorrow.

THE NOTICE BOARD

The following jokes can be played at the office either by putting a notice to all in the canteen or lunch room or they may be emailed to friends and colleagues in other offices who suffer the same indignities as you do.

NOTICE TO ALL EMPLOYEES

Restroom Trip Policy

A Restroom Trip Policy will be established to provide a more consistent method of accounting for each employee's restroom time and ensuring equal opportunity for all employees.

Under this policy a 'Restroom Trip Bank' (RTB) will be established for each employee. The first day of each month, employees will be given twenty (20) RTB credits.

These credits may be accumulated indefinitely.

Within two weeks, the entrance doors to all restrooms will be equipped with personnel identification stations and computer-linked voice print recognition devices. Each employee must provide two copies of voice prints—one normal and one under stress.

Employees should acquaint themselves with the stations during the initial introduction period.

If an employee's RTB balance reaches zero, the doors to the restroom will not unlock for that employee's voice until the first of the next month.

In addition, all restroom stalls are being equipped with timed paper roll retractors and pressure sensitive seats. If the stall is occupied for more than three minutes an alarm will sound. Thirty seconds after the sounding of the alarm, the roll of paper will retract into the wall, the toilet will automatically flush and the stall door will open. If the stall remains occupied, your picture will be taken.

The picture will then be posted on the bulletin board and the first of no more than two official warnings will be issued. If a person's picture appears for a third time, it will be grounds for immediate termination.

All supervisors have received advanced training on this policy. If you have any questions, please ask your supervisor.

NOTICE TO ALL EMPLOYEES

Code phrases
What you say—and what you mean to say:

It has been brought to the management's attention that some individuals have been using foul language. Due to complaints from some of the easily offended employees, this conduct will no longer be tolerated.

The management does, however, realise the importance of each person being able to express feelings properly when communicating with fellow employees. Therefore, the management has compiled the following code phrases, in order that the proper exchange of ideas and information can continue.

Old phrase	New phrase
Another fucking meeting.	Yes, we should discuss this.
Ask me if I give a fuck.	Of course I'm concerned.
Eat shit and die.	Excuse me?
Eat shit and die, asshole.	Excuse me, sir?
Eat shit.	You don't say?
He's got his head up his ass.	He's not familiar with the problem.

I really don't give a shit.

It's not my problem.

Kiss my ass.
No bloody way!
Shove it up your ass.
Tell someone who gives a shit.
This job sucks.
Who the hell died and made you boss?

I don't think it will be a problem.
I wasn't involved in that project.
So you'd like my help with it?
I'm not certain that's feasible.
I don't think you understand.
Perhaps you should check.
I love a challenge.
You want me to take care of this?

OLDIES BUT GOODIES

Why, this happens every day!

This joke is a great joke to play if you use public transport to get to school.

You will need several well trained people to play it. Everyone will need to be sure of his/her role.

It certainly makes the other passengers take notice and gives them something to talk about at work and school. The joke is ideal for a group of people and is so much fun to play.

On the morning you have decided to play the joke you get on a bus, tram or train or ferry and sit down.

At the next stop, someone gets on and hands you a tray with the morning newspaper on it.

At the next stop, someone gets on with a glass of juice for you.

At the next stop, someone gets on with a bowl of cereal for you.

At the next stop, someone gets on with a plate of bacon and eggs for you.

By now, the other passengers are staring at you and waiting to see who will get on at the next stop.

At the second last stop, someone gets on, wipes your hands and face and takes your tray away. At your last stop, you stand up and get off, as if this happens to you every morning.

You will need to be good actors to participate and pull this one off and you will need to be well drilled.

Work out which person is going to get on at which stop and with which props.

Make sure everyone has a copy of the timetable and knows exactly what time you will be passing their stop and where you will be sitting.

Start the journey and try to blend in with the other passengers.

As each actor gets on with some food for you, act as if it is the most natural thing in the world to be served breakfast on public transport.

The actors must also be as natural as possible.

As an extra, you can get on the bus in your pyjamas and dressing gown and have some people bring you your clothes during the trip. You can put these clothes on over your pyjamas.

LOOK! UP IN THE SKY

This joke costs nothing, needs no equipment and can have many victims.

That makes it a very good practical joke to play.

You will need a tall building in a busy street and a couple of friends to help you.

Pick a tall building in a busy street.

When there are quite a few people walking past, stand at the bottom of the building and look up at the top.

Have one of your friends walk past and stop near you.

You have to act as if you don't know each other.

Your friend should also look up.

Have another friend walk past and stop and look up.

By now, you should have aroused the interest of people passing by.

Some of the people start whispering and asking each other what is going on.

Over the next few minutes, the crowd grows bigger and bigger.

Rumours start spreading that someone is out on the roof of the building. After about ten minutes, the crowd has become so large that it is holding up the traffic.

Eventually, the crowd does move away.

Many of them watch the television news that night to see if anything dramatic happened.

A COUPLE OF VARIATIONS OF THIS:

Instead of the street, as in the above prank, you can try other locations:

- If you are on a crowded beach, look at the sea and point out into the distance.
- If you are at a sporting event, stand up and look at a point several rows behind you.

THE WET DOOR

Try the old reliable bucket of water on top of the door joke. Place a bucket of water on top of a slightly open door.

Make sure that the bucket is fastened to something so that it tips when the door opens, but does not fall. You do not want a full bucket of water to drop on someone's head.

FLOUR INSTEAD

Place a bag full of flour on top of a slightly open door. When the victim opens the door, the bag will fall on their head, causing a great mess. Make sure the bag is not too heavy. You don't want to knock anyone out.

PING PONG DOOR

Balance a row of ping-pong balls along the top of a slightly open door. When the victim pushes the door, the balls will fall all over the place.

THE TISSUES JUST KEEP COMING JOKE

Open the box of tissues and take out every single tissue. The easiest way to get the tissues out is by opening the box at the bottom.

Make sure that you keep the tissues folded up, otherwise they will be very hard to put back into the tissue box.

Take the bottom edge of the top tissue and glue it to the top edge of the second tissue.

Take the bottom edge of the second tissue and glue it to the top edge of the third tissue.

Repeat this process until you have glued the second last tissue to the last tissue.

Replace the tissues back into the box, with the top edge of the top tissue poking out of the top of the box.

Tape or glue the bottom of the box so that the tissues won't fall out.

Place the box where it can be easily seen and reached.

Stand back and watch the fun.

WOULD YOU LIKE TO KISS MY MAGIC RING?

Make up a story about how someone in your family was helped by kissing the magic ring that is on your finger.

Tell your friend that the ring has been in your family for hundreds of years and that it is a magic ring.

Say that if he/she makes a secret wish and then kisses the ring while blindfolded, a wish will be granted.

When he/she agrees to do this apply a blindfold.

Say some magic words and ask him/her to think of a wish.

While you are saying the magic words, swap the ring with a lemon quarter tied to a piece of string or an elastic band.

When the victim kisses the lemon it will leave him/her with a sour taste in the mouth.

FROTH AND BUBBLE

This is an easy joke to play and it is also so much fun. However, keep a mop handy for this joke.

It will be needed to clean up.

You will need a bottle of washing up detergent and a toilet.

This is not the joke to play at Grandma's house!

Pour the entire contents of the detergent bottle into the toilet bowl.

Do not flush the toilet. It is the flush that sets the detergent off.

Wait for the victim to go to the toilet.

The victim goes to the toilet. Everything seems normal until they flush the toilet.

Suddenly, soapsuds are overflowing from the toilet bowl.

The soapsuds flow down the side of the toilet bowl and onto the floor.

It is like a horror movie, with monster suds emerging from the sewer.

FOUNTAIN VARIATION

Instead of a toilet, as in the above prank, you can put the detergent into a fountain and watch the suds develop.

Check to see that there are no fish in the fountain first. Never put detergent in a fountain that contains fish.

We wouldn't want to kill the fish, now, would we . . .?

HOSPITAL TRICK

This is an old gag that has become an urban legend.

That is, nobody actually knows somebody that it has happened to, but we all know of somebody that it happened to.

To play this you will need to be in hospital so that limits opportunity. Still, it is a good joke for a laugh.

When the nurse brings you one of those funny-shaped vessels used for urine specimens, asking you to wee in it when it is convenient, bide your time.

When no-one is watching put apple juice in the jar.

When the nurse comes back to collect it—hopefully when there are a few other people around—pick up the sample, hold it up to the light and say, 'This doesn't look right, I think I'll run it through my body again.'

Drink the specimen.

HEALTH REGIME

If you are not in hospital but want to try a version of the urine trick, convince your friend that you are trying a new health regime where you drink a glass of your own urine every day.

Your friend will be doubtful, but to convince him/her that this is what you do invite him/her to your place to watch you.

Hide a bottle of apple juice in the bathroom.

Tell your friend that you need to go to the bathroom to take a urine sample.

While you are there pour apple juice into the sampler jar.

Bring it out to your friend, show him/her.

Ask him/her does he/she want a sniff or a taste.

Your friend will pull a face in distaste and refuse.

Say, 'Cheers!' Hold the glass in the air and then drink it down.

THE DISMANTLE JOKE

Many of the funniest practical jokes are a variation on the theme of dismantling something large and then reassembling it in someone's office/apartment/bedroom.

There is a story about the Volkswagen Beetle fan that, on his birthday, came to work to find a perfect Volkswagen sitting on the floor of his office.

His work mates had disassembled it and then painstakingly reassembled it in his office.

He was utterly at a loss for words, as he couldn't understand how it had come through the door, let alone climbed the stairs.

He left it there and worked around it!

KIDNAPPED!

An old favourite practical joke involves the kidnapping of some small beloved object (teddy bear, pillow, blanket, etc.).

Once this object has disappeared and before its owner has noticed it's gone, suspend it from a window in a public place.

The owner will recognise it and slowly it will dawn on him/her that the precious object is no longer in the place it should be.

HAVING A GREAT TIME, WISH YOU WERE HERE

A much-played variation of this theme is the one where a garden gnome disappears from a garden.

The owners do not know where it is and look for it. In the end they decide that it has been stolen and go about their lives.

In a couple of weeks they receive a postcard from some exotic place.

It has a photo of the gnome enjoying himself—on the beach, in a bar, walking up a mountain or whatever it is that the place is known for—with the message, 'Wish you were here. Having a great time'.

This continues at regular intervals for several months, with the postcards coming from a variety of exotic places and the photographs of the gnome having a good time as if he is on holiday.

Eventually the gnome is returned to the garden from whence he came and the owners go out one day to see him there in his place as if he has been nowhere.

There might be a little packed bag sitting next to him . . .

GOLDFISH IN THE LOO

An ex-cop tells the story of the sergeant who was a stickler for routine. He did everything in a certain way and at a certain time and was loathe to change his habits.

He was such a routine freak that in his 40 years he had only moved out of the regional city where he was born on one occasion and that was to go to the Police Academy to be trained.

As soon as his training was complete, he returned to the town of his birth and stayed there.

Every morning when he turned up for work at 8.50 am to begin his shift at 9.00 am, he would go to the urn, fill a mug with water, dangle a tea bag into it, tuck his paper under his arm and make his way to the toilet where he would sit, complete his ablutions and read the newspaper until 9 o'clock.

On 1 April he was in for a big surprise.

He came into the office and went through his morning routine as usual, but when he closed the toilet door, he let out a howl.

There, swimming around in the toilet bowl, were five fishes!

It ruined his routine and ruined his day.

Here's a similar trick you can play.

Buy two goldfish from the pet shop.

Put the goldfish in the toilet.

A good place to play this one is at your grandparent's place.

ROCK THE CHURCH

Get a clock, set the alarm and place the clock down at the front of the church under the front pew.

You will need to gauge the time it's set to go off so that it erupts in the middle of the service.

Everything will be quiet, the preacher will be droning on in a monotone and all of a sudden the congregation will think that they have died and gone to hell when the piercing alarm breaks the silence.

Of course, don't expect to get your clock back after this trick as you really wouldn't want to own up to it.

A TRIP TO THE SHOPS

This is an old joke that has been played many times and in many places.

It involves sending a person on an errand that he/she cannot possibly fulfil and you know they will be coming back empty-handed.

It is great fun watching them try to do it.

Some things you could order:

- a metric hammer
- a left-handed hammer
- a tin of striped paint
- a tin of spotted paint
- smooth sandpaper
- a straight hook
- invisible ink
- a left-handed screw driver.

HEY, EVERYTHING'S OKAY!

It is amazing that this joke works because it seems so silly. However, you'll be surprised how easily people are fooled.

This joke can be played on anyone that you see riding a skateboard.

As the victim skateboards towards you, gesture towards the back of their skateboard and yell out, 'Your back wheels are going round.'

You haven't told the victim that something is wrong.

In fact you're telling them that everything is okay.

However, the way that you gesture and the tone of your voice suggests that there is a problem.

Stand back and watch the victim as they get off their skateboard and check that everything is okay.

When they realise that there is no problem, they'll probably think back and remember what you said.

Then they'll realise they've been the victim of a practical joke.

Try these other variations:

- For people cycling past on a bicycle, you can call out, 'Your back wheel is going around' or 'Your pedals are turning.'
- For joggers or walkers going past, you can point to their shoes and call out, 'Your shoelaces are done up.'
- For people driving cars or riding motorbikes, you can call out, 'You've got exhaust coming out of the back' or 'Your engine is working.'

WHAT ABOUT THE LUGGAGE?

This joke is best to play on somebody who comes to stay at your house for a holiday.

Usually they bring with them luggage, so this is a good excuse for putting the trailer on the back when you are going to the train station or the airport on their return journey.

You place the victim's luggage on a trailer behind the car.

Make a big thing of tying the luggage down with rope, straps and anything else you can think of.

Tell the victim that the trailer has been playing up a bit lately and that he wants to make sure that the luggage is safe.

The victim gets into the car.

You get in, start the car, rev up the motor, turn up the radio really loud and drive off—and, to the victim's horror, the trailer stays behind.

By this time you are so busy driving the car and listening to his music that you can't hear the victim's warnings that the trailer isn't attached.

You chat away, not hearing the protests.

Of course, eventually you will have to turn around and go back for the luggage or you will miss the plane.

EASY TO DO JOKES

X-Files fans
Create the effect of being abducted by aliens by drinking two bottles of vodka.

You'll invariably wake up in a strange place the following morning, having had your memory mysteriously 'erased'.

Or: edge your lawn into the shape of a pair of trousers, then mow it in lines so it looks like a huge pair of green corduroy trousers. Pockets can simply be added by planting small flower beds.

Townies
Whenever you see country folk driving into town in their green Range Rovers to go shopping, jump up and down screaming, 'Get off my land!' Then shoot their dog.

Phone Messages

When you leave the house simply plug the phone into your video recorder.

Not only will it record the caller's voice, but you will also get a picture of them speaking, probably.

Drive Through Restaurant

Transform your garage into a drive-through restaurant by sitting in your car, lowering your window and demanding that your wife brings you a cup of tea, on roller skates.

Welshman

Pretend to be Welsh by putting coal dust behind your ears, talking gibberish and singing all the time.

Over the Top

To avoid cutting yourself while clumsily slicing vegetables get someone else to hold them while you chop away.

And: help the local police by popping into the mortuary every day to see if you can identify any of the bodies.

Fill a Shredded Wheat with pink soap and, hey presto—an inexpensive Steelo soap pad.

Save money on expensive earrings by sticking Mentos to your ears with Blue-Tack.

Can't afford contact lenses? Simply cut out small circles of cling wrap and press them into your eyes.

Fumes from burning settees can be lethal, so before sitting down always look around and tell everyone you are planning your escape route in the event of a fire.

Save money on expensive personalised car number plates by simply changing your name to match the existing plate.

Avoid embarrassment after tripping in the street by repeating the same movement several times to make it look like a normal part of your behaviour.

Stop flies landing on your dinner by strategically placing a pile of poo on the dinner table. The flies will be so busy munching on the faeces they will leave you to enjoy your meal.

Avoid the morning-after hangover . . . simply stay drunk past noon.

Vegetarians

Hey, vegetarians! Make your veggie burgers go further by adding a pound of mince to them.

Reduce Greenhouse Effects

Save electricity on freezing winter nights simply by unplugging your fridge and placing the contents on your doorstep.

Housewives

When nipping out to the shops, remember to carry a stiff broom in the boot of your car.

Use it to sweep the broken glass to the side of the road every time you have a minor accident.

Bomb Disposal Experts' Wives
Keep hubby on his toes by packing his lunchbox with plasticine and an old alarm clock.

Bus Drivers
If driving a bus is what you do for a living, play this joke on your passengers.

Pretend you are an airline pilot by wedging your accelerator pedal down with a brick, securing the steering wheel with some old rope and then stroll back along the bus, chatting casually to the passengers.

If someone looks stressed, say. 'That ol' auto pilot has never let me down yet!'

Blind Relatives
Increase blind people's electricity bills by switching all their lights on when their guide dog isn't looking.

Doing a Runner
A little known fact about the stuff that makes sore eyes feel good is that it not only clears your eyes up, but if ingested, also clears your colon out too!

Put a few drops of it in someone's drink and it will give them terrible diarrhoea! It's clear so they will never notice.

DUST EVERYWHERE

Take a container of talcum powder, flour or even lots and lots of dust.

You will also need a leaf blower or even a powerful vacuum like a shop vac.

Take a thin piece of cardboard and use it to place the powder as far under the door as you can. Fire up the vacuum cleaner!

Work that nozzle back and forth and make sure that pile of dust/talcum you shoved under the door is blown all away.

Use the vacuum to clean up as much evidence as you can outside the door so there is no sign of what you have been up to.

The powder will cover everything.

It's quite a mess and difficult to clean.

By the way, before you go through this whole set-up, check first to make sure the door is not in fact unlocked . . .

WHAT HAS HAPPENED HERE?

A vacationing neighbour is a great victim for this number. It works even better if said neighbours are leaving the kids behind.

Get yourself a roll of 'Police Line—Do Not Cross' tape.

Then get some dark red paint.

All you have to do is put up the tape across the front of the house and drip some of the fake blood on the front steps and around the doorknob.

When seen by your average person, this should instantly throw the person into a very uncomfortable state.

GLITTER TRAP

The joke victim sits at a desk, pulls out a drawer. A string runs from the back of the drawer, up the wall, into the false ceiling, over to a spot directly over the subject's head, where it triggers the trap: a mousetrap whose action snaps a card away from its position covering a funnel, releasing a handful of glitter, which flows down the funnel, through its spout, through a hole in the ceiling acoustic tile, onto the subject.

It is wonderful to hear a muffled snapping noise and a quiet 'chuff', and watch the slow, glittery descent of a cloud of brightly coloured dust settling over the head and shoulders of your target.

TROJAN HORSESHOE

Suspend a wooden horseshoe by a string from the ceiling in the corridor, so that the horseshoe dangles about 5 cm above the top of an upright broom. Most conventional brooms will stand on their straws with a little coaxing.

Attach a sign labelling the horseshow 'wood magnet'.

Watch and enjoy while some people take it at face value.

THE WRONG END OF THE ROPE

For this one you need a rope and a friend.

Get a hold on the rope, while your friend is doing the same.

Tighten the rope around a corner on a building.

Make sure if somebody can see you, they definitely can't see your friend.

Ask a stranger on the street if he would care to help you hold the rope for a few minutes, while you are off to collect something.

Tell the stranger to keep the rope tight and then walk away.

Make sure your friend on the other side of the building is doing the same.

Result: Two strangers are standing on each side of a corner, wondering when you will be back and eventually wondering why they are holding a rope.

Imagine the situation when the two innocent strangers actually meet.

SOMETHING IS WRONG HERE!

If you know somebody who is in love with his car, simply stuff a dead fish up the exhaust system and wait and watch.

A NICE MESS

Take a garbage can, not too large as you will have to carry it, but make sure that it smells.

The can should be half full of garbage.

Fill the rest of the can with water.

Lean it against a door that opens in.

The can should be leaning at about a 15 degree angle.

You get some good stability by resting it between the door and the door jamb.

Either side of the door works.

Either knock or ring the bell and run—or sneak away and wait.

The person opens the door, the can falls in and garbage aided by water comes crashing into the dwelling.

WATER FOUNTAINS

Many schools, shopping centres or parks have a water fountain and most of them have a knob or handle to shoot the water out and a spout.

Take a stir stick or straw and poke a hole into the washer/filter hole so it sticks in there.

Cut the straw so you have 5 cm protruding.

Jam the thing down in deep and aim the straw where you want to squirt the water. Test it out and make sure the straw is in good.

You'll end up squirting people in the eye.

OLD CARS AND TRAFFIC

• Place an old beat up vehicle near the entrance to a building. Remove the wheels and fill it with cement. It's nearly impossible to remove.

• Cut an old wreck in half and weld it together around a flagpole.

- Disassemble an old car and reassemble it on top of a building or in the main lobby of the building.
- Block off a major road using traffic cones or barrels.
- Get some of the jacks used for moving cars around car lots and move all the cars in a lot so that they are about 10 cm apart and impossible to get into or move.
- Fill someone's car or truck top to bottom with snow. (You'll need a shovel most likely.)
- Place a dead fish in an area of the engine that is hard to get to and that will get hot. Jammed under the radiator is just about perfect. After a couple of days the smell just becomes unbearable.
- Jack up a person's car so the wheels are just barely off the ground, but not enough to be noticeable.

SHOCKING

Run a wire from one of the spark plug wires at the distributor cap through the firewall, under the carpet or floor mat and under the driver's seat.

Bare 1/4 inch of the wire and wrap it under the seat so that the bare end is as close as possible to the victim's butt when they are seated in the car.

When they start the car they should get quite a nice charge.

JOKES TO PLAY AT HOME

A STICKY SITUATION

This is a joke that is best played in summer.
You will need some honey and a cloth.

Go to a friend's house but make sure that they are not at home.

Take the honey and put some on the cloth then cover their door with the stuff.

In the morning the bees and/or flies will be swarming all over the door making it hard to clean off.

MALFUNCTIONING KEYBOARD

Simply unplug the keyboard from the back of the home computer.

AUTUMN JOKE

Collect as many leaves as you can from your garden.
You can even offer to rake up your neighbours' gardens so you can get more leaves.

Pack all the leaves into garbage bags.

Empty one of the bags in front of the gate and then add all of the other leaves.

When your Dad gets home and tries to open the gate to bring the car in, he won't be able to see it for leaves.

Repeat the joke the next afternoon and watch Dad go red in the face.

Alternatively, you could wait until dark and empty the leaves that you have raked up in front of your friend's front door.

Next morning when the family goes to open the front door and go to step outside, they are confronted with the largest pile of leaves they have seen in their life.

They have to push and shove the leaves out of the way before they can make their way outside.

SINK FUN

Find a sink that has a sprayer on it and use a rubber band to hold the spray handle down.

Turn it so it faces where a person would stand when they use the sink.

Stand back and wait for someone to use the sink and get a surprise!

'BOILED' EGGS

Serve up eggs in egg cups for breakfast.
Be sure to eat yours first.

The joke is that yours is the only one cooked.

The others get a surprise when they crack theirs to eat and find it is still raw.

UNWANTED MELODY

Obtain one of those little chips that you sometimes get in greeting cards which play a few bars of a well known song when the card is opened.

Pull the chip from the card.

Hide the chip in the pantry so that every time somebody goes in there, they hear the music.

With a bit of luck, it will go on for days and drive people batty.

POP YOUR POOPER

If you remember those little 'snap-pops' that you got at carnivals as a kid, they work great for this.

Place them under the toilet seat and gently lower the seat.

When the person sits, they have no problem going.

BROWNIES

1. Get some dirt and mix it with syrup until it is like the paste of brownie biscuits.
2. Put in a brownie pan and cover with frosting.
3. Serve and watch the person's face as they try to tell you how good they are.

COLOURING YOUR WORLD

When at a friend's house, take a bar of soap from their shower or bath.

Hollow out part of it and fill the hole with red, green or blue food colouring.

Cover the hole with a thin layer of soap formed from what you hollowed from the bar. Place the bar hole-side down in the shower stall and wait for the fun!

ALL TIED UP

This is a joke for little people because only they can fit underneath the dining table.

Be careful not to play this joke on pregnant women, old people, frail people or people with injuries.

You do not want to hurt anyone.

Hide under the dinner table before everyone sits down or sneak under the table without being seen after everyone is seated.

While everyone is eating, very carefully move from one visitor to the next, undoing their shoelaces and tying them to their neighbour's.

When you have worked your way around the whole table, sneak away.

Hide where you can see the visitors fall when they all stand up.

Instead of tying everyone's shoelaces together, you could tie the visitors' shoelaces to the chair legs or even to the table legs.

The fun starts when they stand up to move to another room or to go home.

MASHED POTATOES

Make up mashed potatoes as you would for any holiday, but also buy a head of cauliflower and make up a batch of cauliflower mashed potatoes.

They look the same as regular mashed potatoes, but they taste like cauliflower. Yuk!

Here's how to make them:

Ingredients:
  2 cups cauliflower, finely chopped
  1 tablespoon sour cream or more to taste
  1 tablespoon butter
  Salt and pepper to taste

Directions:
  Steam or microwave cauliflower until very soft.

Put cauliflower in blender or food processor with butter and sour cream, blend.

Add salt and pepper to taste.

Serve hot.

This will make enough for two servings.

Serve it in a smaller container along with the main mashed potatoes or to be extra devious, mix it into part of the regular bowl of mashed potatoes.

Mark the spot so you know which is the right one to use.

This way some of your guests will get regular, some a mix and some just cauliflower.

COCA COLA

If your friend is drinking Coke or another dark drink and they leave the table briefly, decant their drink into another container.

Then fill their glass with some water and enough soy sauce to make it look like the other drink. You could also add some of their previous drink for the carbonated 'fizzy' effect.

When they return to take a drink it will taste disgusting and they'll need to wash out their mouth, so give them back their original drink!

TASTY SULTANA

Find a dead fly and pull off its wings, legs etc. so only its body is left. Then put it in a packet of raisins!

WATER ANYBODY!

Ask your friend if they would like a drink of water, but instead give them PowerAde. The sudden fizz will surprise them!

MOVING OBJECTS

Choose a number of objects that are easily moved in the room that will be used. It can be a conference room, a lecture theatre or an office.

Do not choose fragile objects that will break if they fall.

The objects must have a part that a piece of fishing line can be tied to.

Cut the fishing line into as many pieces as you need.

Tie one piece of fishing line to each object.

Run the fishing line to a place where you will be able to sit without being seen.

Make sure the fishing line is not visible.

Run it under rugs, next to walls and across mantelpieces.

Go into your hiding place and every now and again give one of the lines a small tug. Do not pull too hard.

You don't want to make the movement too obvious.

Enjoy the look on the faces of the assembled people who think they are seeing things.

They are not quite sure that they are seeing it, so they will say nothing.

No one will be game to say anything as they will think that the others may think that they have Alzheimer's disease or that they are going balmy.

FAVOURITE SPOON

You can play this joke whenever one of your friends pops in for a cup of tea or coffee.

But don't play it on the same person twice.

Buy an old teaspoon from a second-hand shop or use an old one from home.

Grab the oval end of the teaspoon with one hand and, holding it tightly with the other hand, wriggle the oval end until you feel it loosening.

It will eventually break off.

When it has broken off, get a tiny piece of chewing gum and stick the two pieces back together.

Make sure that the gum cannot be seen.

You only need enough to stop the spoon breaking when it is picked up.

Then ask your friend whether she would like a cup of coffee or tea.

Make the hot drink and put the spoon in it.

It has to be a hot drink because the heat will melt the gum.

The victim will add milk and sugar to the coffee and stir it.

As she stirs sugar or milk into her drink, tell her that the spoon is your favourite because it was given to you by a very special friend.

When she takes the teaspoon out, she will be left with only the handle—the bottom part has fallen off.

She will have no idea how it happened, but will feel very embarrassed.

FUN WITH UMBRELLAS

This trick can only be done on a rainy day or night.

Watch to see if any of your colleagues or friends has brought an umbrella with them.

If they did, then you can begin preparing the joke.

Bide your time and when everyone is occupied, open the end of each umbrella and pour lots of confetti inside.

Close each umbrella back up.

Clean up any confetti that you may have dropped.

You don't want anyone getting suspicious.

You might like to put an egg inside the umbrella. It will splatter on the ground.

Put ping-pong balls inside the umbrella, they will bounce everywhere.

Put talcum powder inside the umbrella and turn the visitor's hair white.

Put a plastic spider inside the umbrella and give the visitors a fright.

PUZZLE PUZZLER

That 1000-piece jigsaw puzzle that someone is working on at the dining room table?

When no-one's looking, take one piece from the box and hide it!

You will drive the puzzler crazy.

POOR POP

This is especially good to carry out on your grandpa.

Get up early to get the newspaper.

Have a copy of yesterday's paper and replace the middle of today's paper with yesterday's.

Watch as dear old Pop can't find the continuation of that cover story!

JOKES TO PLAY AT THE OFFICE

TIME PLEASE

When you spot someone carrying a cup of tea or coffee in the hand as they wear their watch, simply ask them what the time is!

KEEPS ON RINGING

Using tape, tape down the rocker on someone's phone, so that when it is lifted it keeps on ringing. This is really funny when your friends start saying, 'Hello can I help you . . . eh?'

SECRET MESSAGES

Find out when your victim is making copies to send to the boss. Before they do, put a piece of clear tape on the glass window of the photocopier with something along the lines of, 'I'm stealing office supplies' or, 'Secret Government Bomb Blueprints' or, if you really want the person to suffer, try something like, 'Mr (boss's name) is a complete ass,' written on it.

COLLAPSING CABINET

Remove the screws that hold the filing cabinet handles on and then stick them back with Blue Tack. Watch the surprise on your co-worker's face, when they go to open the drawer and are stunned after regaining their balance.

DAY TO DAY GAGS

- Put your garbage can on your desk and label it 'IN'.
- Develop an unnatural fear of staplers.
- In the memo field of all your cheques, write 'For sexual favours'.
- As often as possible, skip rather than walk.
- dontuseanypunctuation

IMPRESS THEM

When you are with someone buying lunch at the fast food, specify that your drive-through order is 'to go'.

SPLIT SCREEN

Go put into the car-park, cut a baseball in half and get some cling film, then put the ball on top of the cling film and place on the boss' car's windscreen—hide in the bushes and watch his reaction!

MR BEAR

Leave a message for a co-worker that a 'Mr Bear' called for them. Write down the number for the local city zoo as the phone number to call.

MUSIC CHIPS

Obtain one of those little chips that you sometimes get in greeting cards which play a few bars of a well known song when the card is opened.

Pull the chip from the card.

Place it in the ear piece of a colleague's telephone.

VOICE RECOGNITION

Send official looking memos to all the employees in a department telling them that their computers have had voice recognition software installed.

Tell them they will also be able to operate the entire system by simply speaking.

See how many of them start spelling out their password into the microphone!

SIMPLE BUT VERY EFFECTIVE

If you have two office doors opposite each other, take a piece of string and tie it round both door handles while someone is inside one of the rooms.

However, be very careful doing this!

PIGMENTATION

Y ou can add food colouring to the soil of a potted plant for some rather weird pigmentation.

PHONE PRANK

T his prank works best if your victim has a black phone.
Go to your office copier and open up the area where you add the toner; there is usually some residual toner there.

Rub as much toner as you can collect on your fingers/hand.

Put the toner on the ear piece, mouth piece and/or handle of your victim's phone.

If your prank is successful, your victim will be walking around the office with toner on their ear, cheek and hand.

Be aware that toner cannot be cleaned from clothes.

Perhaps it is kinder to get some hand lotion or thick hair gel and put it on the ear piece of your victim's phone.

When he/she answers their phone or makes an outgoing call, he/she will be totally grossed out, not knowing what that gooey stuff is in his/her ear.

HOT SHOT

C all some you know, disguising your voice and tell them that there is a serious fault with the phone system and that they must not make or answer any calls for the next five minutes.

Warn them that if they do, the person on the other end of the line could be electrocuted.

Call back in a couple of minutes, when they answer scream, 'AARGH' into the receiver and let the line go dead!

MAYHEM

Stay on late at work and divert all the lines into the office to just one phone!

NEW EMPLOYEE

Tell the new employee that the management at a close-by business wants exactly 47 nachos on every tray and they'll get upset if the victim doesn't do it.

Send a new employee for various mythical items such as:

- double sided transparencies
- dehydrated water
- bucket of compressed air
- a one molar solution of water
- a stanchion remover
- a bucket of steam
- a philologian tube
- a long weight (long wait)
- a short weight
- short circuits
- lightning bolts
- skyhooks
- a 'mattababe' (as in what's a 'mattababe')
- a 'dickfore' (same as above)
- a piston return spring
- a left handed wrench, hammer, razor . . .
- agent orange (paint colour)
- a short/long stand
- a chain stretcher
- hydraulic cement blender.

MONDAYS

Brighten up dull Monday mornings at work by concealing a bottle of vodka in your jacket pocket and taking swigs from it at regular intervals throughout the day.

MESSAGES FROM THE LOO

You need: one roll of toilet paper and a marker pen.

Take your roll of toilet paper and unroll it or just part of it, then write on some of the sheets several clever toilet jokes.

For example, 'HELP! I'm trapped in a toilet paper factory!'

Roll it back up and replace the old roll with this one—stand back and wait!

WATER DOWN THE TROUSERS TRICK

At the workplace you and several friends fill your morning coffee cups with cold water and stand around while one guy sticks a funnel in the top of his pants and holds a coin.

When the unsuspecting victim walks in, the funnel guy starts rolling the coin down and off the end of his nose, purposely missing the funnel.

When the victim asks what is happening you tell him you're trying to catch the coin in the funnel.

Invariably the victim will say, 'That's easy' or 'That shouldn't be hard to do.'

You respond with, 'Oh yeah, bet you can't get it in six tries.'

As soon as he sticks the funnel in his pants and tilts back his head, everybody reaches out and dumps their cup of water down the funnel.

With a little planning and practise missing the funnel, this joke will pull off without a hitch and is simply hilarious.

A GOODBYE GIFT

Is your company about to ask you to 'seek other opportunities': in other words, fire you?

Or, are you looking for one last way to let your landlord know he has been horrible all the time you have been staying in his stinky apartment and paying outrageous rent? Maybe, looking to strike back at a car rental agency for a little bait and switch?

We know—would you like to get back at a soon-to-be former love interest?

Then this is the prank for you!

Buy some fish and place it in a tray.

You can even drop in a trout with scales and everything.

Hide the fish behind a drawer or behind a ceiling tile, in a wheel well, under a bed. Make it someplace where it will not be discovered right away.

If you cannot find a dead fish, a can of tuna with holes punched in the top will do the trick as well.

In a few days, nature will start to exact your revenge.

The smell will begin permeating the location, but it will be very hard to locate the source of the smell.

GETTING BACK FOR GETTING THE SACK

Have you ever had a manager that was a complete jerk?
Since a good Wanted Ad will generate at least 400 responses for a job, why not place a bogus Wanted Ad for a job?

Get the direct line, email address and snail mail address for your victim.

If you want to be truly evil, use the exact same job title.

Then write an ad like this:

Office Assistant Needed Looking for a go-getter to help Manager perform routine office duties.

Candidates should be verbally articulate, creative, self-motivated, but we'll train the right person.

Excellent remuneration package. Share options available. Childcare onsite.

Send resume to: Mr (Put his real name), Manager (Address, Website, Email address.)

Post the ad on job bulletin boards and internet sites, in fact, any list you can get away with that costs nothing and where you have to give out very little personal contact information.

You want to make it hard to trace this back to yourself.

The ad will be so good, he will be inundated with applications that he will have to deal with.

SHOWER

Fill someone's umbrella with talcum powder, hole punch waste . . . creating a sudden shower when opened!

IMPOSSIBLE ERRAND

Have you ever had a co-worker on a job site that does more damage than good?

I know how annoying these people can be and sometimes you can't just go up to the foreman and have them fired, since they are the boss' nephew or something just as useless.

Here is yet another way to get rid of them for a while.

Call the new co-worker over and tell them the piece of wood you are working on is too short and you need a board stretcher.

Tell him to run over to a tool and machine rental place and pick one up.

This is how you can tell if the rental guy has a good sense of humour.

See if they refer your co-worker to another rental place.

With any luck, you can have the co-worker driving around all day long looking for a board stretcher.

CARPENTER'S REVENGE

So, you are on the job with a new guy and he claims to be a hot shot, but is he really? One good way to start is to explain to the crew that one of the problems they have with their framing hammer is that it is a left handed hammer, not a right handed hammer. That would explain why their elbow gets a bit sore.

If they are left handed, well, they have a right handed hammer, not a left handed one. Remember, the more people you can get to convince the hotshot his hammer is defective the better.

This also works with saws, screwdrivers or paint brushes.

SAVING ELEVATOR TIME

Do you work in an office in a high rise where you have to use an elevator?

This prank is for you!

Post a sign that due to excessive elevator use, one floor trips cannot be made without an Elevator Pass.

Make up several passes and pass them out to friends to get them in on the deal.

Try to make them the same size as your current passes or ID cards so they look like they fit.

Follow up with an actual form you need to fill out to get an elevator pass.

Post notices wherever you usually post notices to make it seem more official.

Really feeling gutsy?

Spread the notices out to businesses that are not even on your floor.

STUCK ON YOU

Staple an unimportant paper to a desk.
Watch with glee as the victim tries to pick it up and tidy it.

DRUG SIGNS

Place 'Don't do Drugs' signs all over the workplace.

WHO DID THAT?

Walk up to the boss and as you walk by have a whoopee cushion in your pocket and squeeze it.

Make sure that you look innocent, as if this is an everyday situation for you and no cause for embarrassment what-so-ever.

The really brave prankster will let out a genuine fart.

INKY MESS

Take an exploded pen and replace it on your co-worker's desk amongst his/her pens. You will not be popular as ink will go everywhere.

WHERE DID I PUT THAT?

Re-organise a person's office so that everything is in a different place.

Put the desk in the opposite side, the paintings on the another wall, the filing cabinet in another corner and so on, so that when he walks in next morning, he thinks he is in the wrong office.

MOVING STORY

Reposition the monitor of a co-worker's computer every day for a week.

Slightly rearrange his/her desk so that he/she is not quite sure that tricks are being played.

Eventually, after a series of moves, move the monitor right off the desk and onto the floor.

IMMOVABLE OBJECT

Super-glue a co-worker's stuff to the desk, then when he or she tries to get a pencil or some thing off her desk she won't be able to move anything.

USELESS STUFF

Fill an empty white out bottle with milk and replace it on your co-worker's desk. He/she will not understand why it is not doing as it is supposed to do.

MONSTER

Put a live lobster or any other creature in the file cabinet. This is sure to bring hysterical reactions.

VOLUME

If a computer has speakers turn the volume all way up or way down depending and have a giggle watching the reaction.

ANNOUNCEMENT . . .

Grab the intercom and in your best possible stage voice intone, 'Elvis has left the building. Ladies and gentlemen, Elvis has left the building . . .'

Announce that, 'The parking attendant is in the car park, slapping $100 fines on everyone's car.'

Announce that, 'Would the last person leaving tonight, please turn the lights out, as we are closing the business forever and no-one need come to work tomorrow.'

FRIES WITH THAT?

Every time someone asks you to do something, say, 'Certainly, m'am,' and ask, 'Do you want fries with that?'

AEROBICS

Encourage your colleagues to join you in a little synchronized chair dancing.

RUBBISH

Put your garbage can on your desk and label it 'IN'.

I NEEDED THAT!

Put decaf in the coffee maker for three weeks.
Once everyone has gotten over their caffeine addictions, switch to espresso.

ANNOYING

Reply to everything someone says with, 'That's what you think.'

AMEN

Finish all your sentences with 'In accordance with the prophecy'.

BRIGHT SPOT

Adjust the tint on your monitor so that the brightness level lights up the entire work area. Insist to others that you like it that way.

TWINS

Find out where your boss shops and buy exactly the same outfits. Wear them one day after your boss does.
This is especially effective if your boss is of the opposite gender.

IMPORTANT PERSON

Send e-mail to the rest of the company to tell them what you're doing.

For example, 'If anyone needs me, I'll be in the bathroom, in Stall #3.'

BITTEN

Put mosquito netting around your cubicle.

MUSIC

Play a tape of jungle sounds all day.

VOICES

Tell your boss, 'It's not the voices in my head that bother me, it's the voices in your head that do.'

CONSTANT RING IN MY EARS

Tape down the switch hook buttons on a phone and get some interesting reactions. When the receptionist rings that number to put a call through, the phone will keep ringing and she will not know what is happening.

TALK BACK

Program co-worker's phone to forward to the office paging system. Sit back and listen while his/her calls are broadcast for all to listen to.

RUMOURS

Ask your co-worker, 'Are you really going to be fired or is that just a rumour?'

RANSOM

Does your co-worker have a special personal ornament or photograph in the office? Take it and leave a ransom note demanding a certain set of circumstances for it to be returned at a certain time and in a certain and slightly sinister manner.

LUNCH SWITCH

If a co-worker brings a bag lunch, switch the contents.
It's even better if you switch it to something totally random and different. For example you could replace his sandwiches and fruit with a can of beer and half a dozen condoms.

SWITCHBOARD CONFUSION

Pull the labelled buttons off a co-worker's phone and rearrange the order. Put them back on their phone.

They won't be sure of which line is which or which connects them to the boss!

HEAVY HANDLE

Tape your victim's telephone receiver down at top and bottom when they are away from their desk.

When they come back, call them from your desk and watch them struggle to answer.

BLURRY FIGURES

Put transparent tape over the read out of a calculator.
It makes the numbers blurry.

AWARD

If your boss wins some kind of prestigious award, manufacture a phoney memo from the company president announcing that the award has been discontinued.

SPILT MILK

Buy a package of approximately 200 of those little paper bathroom cups and neatly arrange them all over the subject's desk. Then staple them all together and fill them with water. See how long it takes them to figure out how to get rid of this set-up without spilling water all over everything.

PHOTOCOPIER

Take the paper out of the copier and write, 'Everything written on the flip side of this paper is a lie!'

Put it back into the copier mixed with regular sheets.

WRONG LABEL

Take one of your co-worker's 3 1/2 floppies and label it with something banned at your workplace.

DRAFTSMEN

It is common for draftsmen to sprinkle Scumex (powdered rubber eraser) on tracings prior to doing any drawing on it.

This reduces smearing of the pencil marks and such and results in a cleaner tracing.

A group of draftsmen replaced the Scumex at their colleague's desk with dried parmesan cheese.

It looked about the same.

It was extremely interesting watching him draw for a while and then begin to smell the paper.

Took the poor guy almost 10 minutes to guess that he had been gagged!

HEARING VOICES

Buy a voice changer at a toy store and answer the phone in strange voices.

WRAPPED UP

Seal the boss's desk during his/her vacation in plastic wrap.

VALERIAN ROOT

Get Valerian root capsules (available at health food stores) and when co-worker is away from desk, take his phone apart and open a capsule or two of Valerian root in the mouthpiece then replace.

Guaranteed to smell terrible!

NOT SO TASTY

At lunch, swap the worker's real food with look-a-like dog toy food.

UPSIDE DOWN

Many desk drawers have a board under them so that you can take the drawer out.

Remove the contents, put the drawer back in, but upside-down!

Then, while the upside-down drawer is partially opened, put the contents back in and close it.

When the unsuspecting victim opens the drawer, all the contents fall out!

PROBLEM SOLVED

If able to impersonate your supervisor's voice, call co-worker and have them write incident report/memo on 'their problem'.

Watch as they turn it in.

NON SMOKING POLICY

If you work in a building that has a non smoking policy, buy a carton of (soft pack) cigarettes, an ashtray and stay really late one night.

Place the ashtray on the victim's desk.

Light up about five cigarettes and place them in the ashtray.

Throw away the rest of the cigarettes but keep the packs.

Crumple them up and toss them all over the victim's office/cubicle.

GLUED ON

Take some cellophane and open up the glue bottle.
Put the cellophane across the opening, then close the bottle.
Watch the victim try to squeeze glue out.
They either open it up to check or they squeeze too hard, breaking the cellophane and spraying glue everywhere.

DAY OFF

Tell a new worker that everyone has tomorrow off because of the boss's religious beliefs.
See if he shows up the next day.

COVER UP

Take a small spray bottle and fill it with water.
Pretend to sneeze and spray the person who sits in front of you in the back of the neck.
Hide the bottle and cover your mouth with your hand as if you are covered in snot.`
Apologise and hold out your hand to shake hands.
Alternatively, wipe your wet hand on his/her shirt.
After five minutes, do it again . . .

IS THAT THE TIME?

Gather up a lot of alarm clocks and set them to go off at various times throughout the day in different places.
Then simply wait for reactions.

WHO ARE YOU?

If someone goes off on vacations, when he/she gets back, treat him/her as if he/she were a visitor or a new fellow on the block.

Confusion guaranteed.

GOT CALLER ID?

Next time your phone rings and if you recognise the caller's name or phone number, answer it saying, 'Hello, may I speak to (use a wrong name)?'

Afterwards, your caller will get confused and tell you that you have the wrong phone number.

Then they'll call back, but do this about three times (if they haven't caught on or given up) and after the third time they call you, ask for their name, they will be totally confused.

You can have a lot of fun with this joke.

You can even pretend to be a credit card company representative or even a telemarketer.

NEW STAFF

When you have a new secretary on board make a call saying, 'This is the phone company. We are testing a new circuit wiring scheme in your offices. Please keep everyone off the phones for the next 10 minutes. We will be verifying the correct wiring of your system by passing hot steam through the wires. Instruct your employees to place their phones on the floor or, better yet, wrap them in towels to avoid scalding themselves. We will advise you when the tests are complete.'

Wait and watch.

STOLEN SUPPLIES

First, steal everyone's office supplies, including yours or you would be looking suspicious.

Take the supplies (i.e. staples, pencils, tape, white out, etc.) and hide them.

Leave messages on their desks announcing that there will be a treasure hunt to retrieve the supplies.

CAN'T HEAR YOU

When talking other the phone in a busy office keep saying, 'What?' and see how loud the person on the other end will last before giving up. You could even draw up a league table!

JOKES TO PLAY IN A PUBLIC TOILET

HOW TALL ARE YOU?

Use the toilet stall in a public men's room to take a leak. Take off your boots, place them by the toilet so as to look like you're still standing in them and stand with stocking feet on the toilet to do your business.

People are amazed to see a nine foot man taking a leak, because all they see is your boots down at the bottom of the stall and the top half of your body.

A SHOCKING BUSINESS

Go into a men's bathroom that has urinals. Simply put the 9 volt battery into the urinal and let it sit for about 5–10 minutes.

After that time whenever a person urinates in the urinal it will deliver a shocking sensation.

WATERY

On a cubicle where the door reaches the floor, seal the door shut and fill the cubicle with water. You may wish to introduce marine life.

NO ESCAPE

When someone is in a bathroom stall, duct tape him in or wedge something against the door so that he cannot get out.

If you are feeling really mean, wee on the floor so he will have to crawl through the urine to escape under the door.

STRAINED LOOKS

When you see someone taking a dump in a stall, go into the stall right next to him and put a mirror down between the two stalls.

It is so funny to see the guy's face after you do this.

COLD COMFORT

Make a hole in the back of a porta-loo.

When someone sits on the seat put a water pistol gun tip through the end.

Fire away!

THE OLD EXPANDING FOAM TRICK

All that you will need for this is a can of expanding foam.

Go to a public or school bathroom and bring a can of expanding foam with you.

Go into a stall and open the can.

Now spray the foam into the bowl of the toilet until it is about 3/4 of the way full.

Write a sign on the stall door saying, 'This toilet is currently getting fixed, please do not use.'

Tape it to the door and lock the stall.

Wait for a few hours, then go back and take the sign off and unlock the stall.

The foam will have started to become solid.

The next person who goes to the bathroom will have a mess to deal with.

Then, when he flushes, the toilet will flood.

BUBBLES

Pour a load of bubble bath liquid in the tank of a toilet so it foams up when flushed.

ITCHY-POO

Cover the first layer of toilet paper with itching powder.

A GOOD READ

Take all the toilet paper away and leave them with some newspaper.

TAKEN FOR THE RIDE

Take a long chain and a car.
Hook the chain on to a porta-loo and drag it down the highway with someone inside.

BUTTERED TOILET SEATS

Butter all of the toilet seats. And while you are at it, also butter doorknobs.

FLOODING THE TOILET

Wrap plastic wrap over the toilet bowl then replace the seat. This one can be really messy!

YUK!

Sprinkle flour on the floor of the shower. It gets wet and looks like someone has been wanking in there.

SPURT

Fill some surgical tubing with water and, holding both ends carefully so that the water does not escape, put the tube in the victim's desk drawer and jam the ends, so that they are sealed.

When the draw is opened it will release the tube and water will spurt everywhere.

APPLE JUICE, ANYBODY?

Pee in a bottle and leave it around in an apple juice container. Offer it to someone as a drink.

BLUE URINE

Take a syringe (with needle preferred) and fill it with a bio-stain known as methane (the gas) blue.

You then inject the dye into your victim's dark-coloured drink.

The effect is that it will turn his/her urine blue.

What terrible disease turns urine blue?

RUDEY, NUDEY

In a gym or public swimming pool, swipe a person's clothes while they are showering.

Put the clothes in an embarrassing place such as the showers for people of the opposite sex.

JOKES TO PLAY IN A SHARED HOUSE

SELF-PEELING BANANA

For this you need a banana (preferably one which isn't ripe yet) and a needle.

Up near the top, pierce through the banana skin with the needle and work it from side to side. This will slice through the banana.

Move down a few millimetres and do it again. Work your way to the bottom, cutting the banana into slices.

If you only make holes in the skin where there are already slight dark patches it will just look like a normal banana.

But when peeled, the banana will, to the great surprise of whoever is eating it, be sliced!

When doing this it is important to use a sterile needle and to give the banana to someone immediately after slicing it (or it will go off where the air has been touching it).

BLUE MILK

Put a tiny drop of blue food colouring in a friend's glass of milk. They will think something is wrong with it!

WHAT ARE WE EATING?

Carefully remove the labels from some tins of food and reglue them on different tins.

Don't do this with all the tins as it will be too obvious.

Watch and laugh.

EXPLOSION

Freeze a can of shaving cream.

When you are sure it is solid inside, saw the top off.

Try not to inhale the aerosol.

Take the frozen shaving cream and place it inside whatever you want to be creamed—a mate's room is usually a great target.

When it thaws it will expand and cover everything in the room!

TAMPON CAPERS

When you have a group of people over and everyone is out in the lounge room, wander off to the bathroom and grab one of your housemate's tapered slim line tampons and use the red food dye you secretly placed there earlier. Start dunking. When it's all plump and red, you are ready.

Loudly come into the lounge room swinging the dripping red tampon like a crazed cowboy.

Wave it at everybody until people start threatening you with death or dismemberment.

For the finale, you've got two choices, either give it one more swing and send it flying into your mate's forehead or stop, wait until everyone calms down then stick it in your mouth and suck on it.

Either way, you probably won't be staying at the house much longer.

JUNK MAIL

Often one must put their name on a list to receive junk mail. Sometimes we don't know that we are doing this, as it may be something as simple as the chance to win a trip away by signing a form in the local fish and chip shop.

Go out of your way to sign a friend up for every piece of junk mail that you can possibly find.

He will suffer an increase in the volume of mail coming to him and gradually it will increase to become a tidal wave.

PING PONG DOOR

This is a prank that can be played in a shared house or residence on an inmate who has a door that opens inwards.

Wait until the inmate is tucked up happily in bed in bye-bye land.

Tape together a bunch of sheets of newspaper to cover the doorframe.

Then tape this big sheet over the doorframe which leaves a gap of about two or three inches between the sheet and the door.

Fill the gap with paper balls right to the top of the doorway.

When your inmate yawns, stretches and opens the door to go to the toilet next morning, he will be showered with a barrage of paper balls, which will make a nice mess!

You may use ping pong balls instead of crushed up newspaper.

LOCKED IN HIS OWN ROOM

Once you have stolen a friend's room keys, the room is yours to plunder.

However, there are more clever ways to have some fun at his expense.

Reverse the lock, so the keyhole faces into the room and then steal the keys.

Challenge your friend to a race back to your room and let him/her win.

Slam the door shut on him/her.

Turn the key and lock him/her into his/her own room.

EXPLODING SALT AND PEPPER SHAKERS

Empty salt (or pepper) from container and fill about 1/3 full with concentrated lemon juice.

Place a thin tissue across the opening, poke it down a bit to form a depression and fill the depression with about a teaspoon of baking soda.

Cover, from the inside, the holes of the top with tape of the appropriate colour.

Replace top on container and trim visible tissue from around the top.

Carry the device to dining table (upright and as stable as is possible, for your own sake).

Discreetly place the shaker on your table.

She/he will shake lightly at first, then harder as nothing comes out.

Due to the breakdown of the tissue and the pressure resulting from the classic acid/base reaction, the top will pop off quite spectacularly amidst a shower of foam. Your victim, as will as everyone around, should have quite a reaction, since you do not usually observe this type of behaviour in a salt (pepper) shaker!

This gag involves an exploding top that will pop off so you must be watchful to ensure that when it does go off it only explodes towards the ceiling.

Carefully observe the person using the salt (pepper) as you may need to grab the shaker from the victim to direct the top towards the ceiling before it goes off. So, watch carefully!

BIRTHDAY PRANKS

Pranks that can be played in residence can often get out of hand. Typically, people are shafted on their birthday, which is therefore a hazardous date to reveal.

Total demolition of a room is quite common, but lacks any real humour.

A common shaft is to remove everything from the birthday person's room and set it up somewhere else exactly as it was.

You could move the entire room to a lecture theatre, a car park or the front yard.

A good idea is to take a digital photograph of the first room so that you set it up exactly as it was.

BIRTHDAY SUIT

If you are in a shared house or a hall of residence, an old faithful trick is to wait until the birthday boy/girl is happily lathering up in the shower.

Sneak in and remove all towels, clothes or anything else that he/she can cover him/herself with.

Then stand by and watch the birthday person streak.

BOUILLON SHOWER

Go to your bathroom and unscrew the shower head.
Use a wrench to loosen the shower head.

Take a slice of bread and shove this into the pipe ahead of the bouillon cubes.

This will keep any dripping water from disintegrating the cubes too soon.

Place a few bouillon cubes into the pipe leading into the wall.

Screw the shower head back in place and wait for the next person to shower.

You may want to use Teflon tape to keep it from leaking.

The bread will dissolve quickly and then the bouillon cubes will start to dissolve.

SNAP POWDER

First you need: iodine crystals and some ammonium hydroxide.
Mix the two together and a brown sludge will form.

Drain off the excess liquid and let the sludge dry.

The result?

Snap powder, a pressure sensitive explosive.

Just sprinkle this on the floor and watch people's reactions as they walk on it and make it snap, crackle and pop.

CAR SPACES

This is a great joke to play on the type of person who is careless with his/her parking and regularly takes up two parking places as he straddles the line making the adjoining park only suitable for a motor bike.

It often happens when parks are tight in a residential zone and every bit of kerb side space is valuable real estate.

You will need a group of muscled young men to lift the car from where it is and to place it somewhere else in an inappropriate position where he/she can't possibly get out of in a hurry or you could turn it upside down on the nature strip.

Write a note on the windscreen saying that you are from the Council and as he/she only has a resident's permit for one car, that in future if he/she wishes to use two car spots he/she will need two resident's permits.

SHAKE HANDS

All you need is vinegar, a cup and an egg.
You put the egg in the vinegar in the cup then wait for about eight hours.

The vinegar will eat away the shell of the egg, leaving it with a thin covering.

You find someone that you would like to tease or get back on, then pretend if you are going to shake their hand in a truce.

Of course, you have an egg in your hand so it will be a mess.

Or another thing you can do is put it on their seat just as the person is about to sit down.

The egg will be very fragile and will pop easily.

TOP SHOT

When your friend is sleeping, place screwed up tissues, a tub of Vaseline and a sign saying, 'Hand jobs for 10 c'.
Take a photo!

MOVING OBJECTS

Every day take a small object from another housemate's room and place it in a different room.
Repeat until room is empty.

DOOR BLOCKER

Pile all of the furniture in your house against someone's bedroom door.

When they wake up in the morning, they can't get out!

MATTRESS OVER

If you want to piss off your room mate, flip their mattress and re-make their bed, so that when they are really tired and just want to crash, they will have to flip their mattress back over and make their bed again!

WRONG NAME

When you meet a friend's girlfriend, say, 'Hello, you must be Susan—I've heard so much about you—he says you're really hot!' when all the time you know full well her name is Jennifer or something.

A ROOMFUL OF TROUBLE

When your housemate or dorm mate is out of the house for a period of hours, this is a great joke to play and to fill a rainy day.

You will need to collect copious newspapers so that you can crumple them up and completely fill his room from floor to ceiling.

When he returns he may not even be able to get into his room at all.

SLEEPING LIKE A BABY

Every night for a week, someone should go in and do something to a given flatmate while he/she is still asleep.

Make sure that it is nothing really nasty.

It may take some time for him to have the realisation that something is going on.

SNOW BUSINESS

Phase 1

When your flatmate/housemate/dorm mate is away from his room, begin to pile up a large amount of snow outside of his window.

If the snow is wet it packs heavily and easily.

On colder days, a hose may be used to harden the snow.

Build a huge pile of snow until it reaches two or three metres.

Go into his room and close his shades and curtain so that he will not notice what you are doing, until it is too late.

Phase 2

Wait for him to come home.

When he arrives and enters his room wait and listen outside his door.

When you hear the shades go up enjoy his reaction as he is confronted with a wall of snow.

At this point, wedge a paperback book between his door and the frame.

Sit back and listen as he starts to try and open the door and, of course, he can't.

He will not be able to go out the window or the door.

Now is the time to get him to agree to help with the household tasks and to be more considerate of others.

GIANT SNOWBALL

Make a giant snowball, remembering that the bigger the snowball, the funnier this trick is. It should be at least one metre in diameter.

Wait until your housemate goes out and then place it in the middle of his room.

If you have to haul the snowball upstairs it will require a team of people to do it.

Turn off the heat in the room and open the windows so that the snowball won't melt too fast.

Wait until the room owner returns.

RAW EGGS

Place raw eggs under the person's pillow or comforter or somewhere else that is bulky enough that the eggs won't be noticed until after they have been crushed.

This is lots of fun to clean up after . . .

FOLDER CREAM

Fill an accordion folder with shaving cream, insert under someone's door and stomp on it, which will send large amounts of shaving cream into their room without ever opening the door.

FOLDER POWDER

A similar trick can also can be done with a fine powder—talcum powder works nicely.

Put it in a bag with a hole in the bottom. Slip the open end under the door, stick a hair dryer in the hole at the other end and the room gets a nice coating.

BURN, BABY, BURN

Hold a magnifying glass over someone who is sunbathing up on the shared house roof.

Be prepared to run shortly after you do this.

HOT NUTS

Place super hot Atomic Balm or the like in someone's jocks or underwear.

Warning! This results in screaming, even with the most macho of guys.

SOBER UP

Hold mayonnaise that has been in the microwave, under the nose of a person who is drunk and feeling queasy.

PURPLE MONSTER

Get some silver nitrate and rub it on your skin. It has the odd effect of turning skin a blackish purple. Sit in the TV room as if nothing has happened.

WALKING MESSAGES

Write all sorts of nasty messages in permanent marker on a person's body while they are asleep or passed out drunk.

Put them in hard to cover up places.

NO SLEEP

Purchase several hundred crickets from the local pet store and release them everywhere.

Crickets are quite noisy and should result in a few sleepless nights.

PRACTICAL JOKES TO PLAY IN PUBLIC

JOKES TO PLAY WITH TECHNOLOGY

Purchase a 'Universal TV Remote' from a place like Radio Shack. When walking by public TVs, such as those in a shopping centre or a pub, change the channel without giving anyone any idea you are doing it.

IN A SHOPPING CENTRE

Make a tiny pin hole in the side of a $5 note and then put some clear fishing line through it.

Sit down and hold the string in your hand.

Whenever someone tries to pick it up, jerk the string.

ZOO CAPERS

When leaving the zoo, start running towards the parking lot, yelling 'Run for your lives, they're loose!'

AM I AT THE RIGHT GAME?

Arrange to go to the football with a friend and his Dad, who support the same team as you do.

In the week before the match, put the blank audiotape in the tape recorder and record shouts for the team that you and your friend do not support.

Vary them and make them annoying and loud.

On the day of the football, hide the tape recorder in a bag so that the victim doesn't know you have it.

Make sure you sit among people supporting the same team as you.

When the victim goes to the toilet or to buy something to eat, take the tape recorder out of your bag, turn the volume right up and place it under or behind the victim's seat, making sure that you are able to press the 'Play' button.

It is a good idea to put the tape recorder behind your friend as it will be easier to press the button.

When there is a quiet moment, press the 'Play' button, so that the tape recorder plays a shout for the opposing team.

Look at the victim in disgust.

Other people will probably do the same.

Repeat this every now and again during the match.

LONG HAIRED GIT

This one is for people with long hair.
Wait until you are in line somewhere where there is a lot of people.

Take a tic-tac and hide it in your hand and start to pick in your hair.

After a few minutes of digging, act like you just pulled a louse out of your hair, then eat it!

People will squirm.

THIS WAY, SIR!

This joke takes quite a bit of setting up, so you will need to be well organised to pull this one off.

It is a great way to welcome a friend home from holiday and to resume the happy relationship that you had before he/she went away.

This trick takes place at an airport, when your friend has just returned from a holiday.

You will need a bicycle, a piece of cardboard with your friend's name written on it and a chauffeur's uniform.

When your friend returns home from the holiday and gets off the plane lounge, he will see a uniformed chauffeur holding a sign with their name on it.

The chauffeur welcomes your friend home and says a limousine is awaiting them outside.

He carries your friend's bags out of the airport and around the corner, where there is nothing but a bicycle.

What a disappointment!

The look on your friend's face will be priceless.

SOMEBODY FAMOUS

To play this joke you will need to organise a group of willing, screaming people who have autograph books and pens.

Make up some specially designed CD covers with your friend's picture on them.

When you know that your friend will be in a public place have a group of screaming and hysterical young boys and girls mob your friend.

They will ask for autographs and want to touch and kiss your friend.

The boys and girls will act as if your friend is the world's greatest pop star.

Your friend will wonder what's going on and will be very embarrassed.

Members of the public will try to catch a glimpse of your friend, whom they assume is a major pop star.

The joke will end when one of the actors calls out a key word that all the others have been told to listen for.

As soon as this word is shouted out, everybody runs away, leaving your friend wondering what's going on.

After the actors have run away, leaving the victim bewildered, you can come out from where you've been hiding and let him know that he/she has been the victim of a practical joke.

ENERGY DRINK

f you are a swimmer this is fun to play.
While your friend is swimming, take his energy drink and drink it all.

Replace it with pool water dyed with food colouring.

He will not know the difference until it is tasted.

Keep well out of the way while you enjoy the joke.

ADDED SPICE

Going to a restaurant can be boring sometimes, but it can be spiced up if you take a Windex or other glass cleaner plastic spray bottle filled with water and a few drops of blue dye.

Use two or three drops of blue food colouring in water to get just the right colour.

Pull it out, spray your food, saying, 'It just doesn't have the zing that I like.'

Unscrew the top and take a couple of mouthfuls and put it back into your briefcase.

It will create a stir.

VOMIT

Go to any gag store and get a fake plastic vomit.
Put it in a drinking fountain.

When wet, it is amazingly realistic . . .

WHAT IS THAT?

Go with a couple of friends, stand near some busy street corner and take a great interest in some point near the top of a tall building or maybe just up in the sky. Watch the reactions of people around you.

RIPPING JOKE

Take an old window shade, go to a gymnastics show or anywhere else where people wear leotards, wait for someone to do a split and tear the window shade briskly, making a very loud ripping sound . . .

BUBBLY FOUNTAIN

Grab a bottle of liquid dish soap and cut off the top.
Dump into a public fountain.

Come back in about 10 minutes and enjoy.

MONEY FOR NOTHING

Superglue a penny in the coin return of a vending machine.
Enjoy watching very well-off people attempting to pry loose
a stupid penny that was never rightfully theirs to begin with.

You can also glue a penny to the floor in front of the vending
machines.

CHANGING CHANNELS

With a Universal remote, stand outside someone's window and flip
the channels.

YUK

Take some potato salad onto the airplane.
Also take a plastic spoon or fork.

Once you are seated, reach into the seat pocket in front of you,
take out the sick bag and put the potato salad into the sick bag.

When the meal is being served, say to the flight attendant, 'No
thanks . . . I've brought my own.'

Then proceed to eat your potato salad.

THINGS YOU CANNOT DO IN PUBLIC PLACES

In New South Wales, Australia, it is legal to relieve yourself in public if
you do it next to the rear left tyre. This goes back to the horse and

buggy days when there was a part of the carriage used for such purposes.

Here are other examples:

- In Chicago, it is illegal to eat in a place that is on fire.
- In Indiana, it is illegal to go to a theatre within four hours of eating garlic.
- In Nebraska, it is illegal to go whale fishing.
- In Lehigh, Nebraska, it is illegal to sell donut holes.
- In Utah, it is illegal for first cousins to marry before they reach 65.
- In France, at least 70% of the music radio stations broadcast must be by French composers.

CUDDLY AND COSY

If you're in a pickup leaving a job site and you happen to be the third guy on the far side from the driver.

When you see a girl, reach over and beep the horn and then duck down.

The girl will look over to see two guys sitting smack up against each other.

PARKING LOT PRANK

Go into a parking lot with a small piece of paper and a pen. Write the following on the paper, 'Sorry about the dent. You were parked awkwardly and I had some problems, but my insurance will cover it. Besides, it's only a small dent, right? Again, sorry.'

Scribble it quickly so it looks like you were in a hurry, but make it readable.

Put it on the nicest car in the parking lot, stand back and wait for the inspection and head scratching to take place.

ATM

When the money comes out of the ATM, scream, 'I Won!, I Won!'

WHOPPER

Go into Burger King and ask for pizza with 'extra whopper'.

I'LL HAVE THAT

At a restaurant or fast food place, ask the price of everything on the menu, then order something you didn't ask the price of!

GOOD NIGHT!

Go into a bedding shop and begin trying out their beds. Come to one that you like and that has been all made up with the pillows and quilts.

Tell the assistant that you really like that one but just to be sure can you please try it out.

He will think that you merely mean to lie on the top of it.

But, oh no, you take off your shoes; drop your daks to show your boxer shorts, carefully fold them and put them on the back of a chair; take off your shirt, get your teddy out of your bag; pull back the covers and hop into bed; snuggle up and go to sleep; if anybody tries to get you out of bed tell them to 'Shush!' as you are trying to sleep and you didn't have a good night's sleep last night.

3D MOVIE

Attempt to enter a movie theatre, showing a normal movie, wearing 3D glasses.

Assure the attendant that they'll work at ANY movie.

OWN COMFY SEAT

Attempt to enter a movie theatre carrying a folding chair under your arm.

This is best if done by a large group.

When they ask, tell them that you prefer this to the theatre chairs.

DANCING IN THE STREET

Gather together several CDs your friends and you love to boogie to, take your boom-box portable CD player and go to the beach on a hot day or perhaps a park.

It is better if you keep away from your own suburb, as you wouldn't want to be recognised.

Another great place to do this would be a busy shopping strip on a Saturday morning.

Set your boom-box up, set the volume to 'loud' and begin to dance.

The more people you can enlist for this prank, the better.

Who knows some of the passers by may even take time out to join in the dance party.

It may put a smile on their faces and make their day!

PARTY COLOUR

At a crowded party or nightclub with a line to the bathroom, crack a glow stick and then snip the end, emptying the glowing contents into the toilet/urinal.

Hilarity ensues when the people behind you are shocked and amazed at your glowing urine!

If someone comments on it, tell them nonchalantly that you used to live near a nuclear power plant.

HOT STUFF

Take one chilli pepper and wait for your victim to set their drink down.

Cut the pepper in half and rub it on the can or cup where your victim places his/her mouth.

Watch as they take a drink and about 2 to 3 seconds later realise that their mouth begins to grow hotter and hotter.

Nonchalantly ask, 'What's the matter?'

BEETLES

Collect beetles from around the outside light.

Take the bag full of live beetles to a parking lot.

The local video store is best, because people are in there for only a few minutes at a time.

Look for a car where the windows are down only a few inches and dump the beetles in there.

Then wait for the owner of the car to come back.

BEACH

Take water guns to the beach and act like you are sleeping in your lounge chair. As people walk by discreetly squirt them but keep your eyes barely open.

HOW MUCH DID YOU SAY THAT WAS?

Wander into a milk bar with a few coins clasped in your hot little hand and order four musk sticks, two gob-stoppers, ten cents worth of mint leaves, ten cents worth of raspberries, five bananas and a liquorice stick.

Wait until the kind lady has put them into a bag and just as she is about to pass them over to you, look worried and ask how much it all comes to so far.

Count your money.

Surprise, you haven't got enough!

Ask her to remove one redskin, three mint leaves, four raspberries and a liquorice stick.

Check how much it all comes to again.

Take your time and be as annoying as possible.

Just as she is about to lose patience, come good with the correct money.

You may never be free to go back into that particular shop again.

FAST FOOD ORDERS

If you work at a fast food drive through window, repeat everything they order in the form of a question.

For instance:

'I'll have a quarter pounder with cheese and fries.'

'Would you like fries with that?'

'Would you like to upsize that to a full quarter pounder?'

'Would you like to add cheese on your quarter pounder?'

Space out the questions so they have time to repeat their order between each inane round of questioning.

TURN AROUND

If you are at the drive-through side of a fast-food speaker, turn things around.

When they ask, 'Would you like fries with that?'

Repeat their question, then say nothing. 'Would I like fries with that?'

Repeat as long as possible.

SUPER MAC

At the McDonald's Drive-Thru order everything with the word 'Mc' in front of it. McCoke, McFries, McQuarter Pounder with McCheese.

Finish with a McJagger.

SHOPLIFTER

If you work in a department store and wish to spice your day up a bit try this gag.

For this, you need to use the large plastic clips that set off the alarm when you exit a store without paying.

Open up the clip on the sensor and remove the shiny piece of paper.

It is about an inch long and about half an inch wide.

This is what actually sets off the alarm and is actually called a 'thingy'.

This 'thingy' is easy to insert into a pen case, or the lining of one of your co-worker's jackets.

Every time that the poor sod walks through the department store door, he will set the alarm off and have some explaining to do.

And. of course, if the 'thingy' is sewn in cleverly enough, he will not have any idea about what is setting it off.

STYROFOAM PEANUTS

Take Styrofoam packing peanuts, paint them with orange poster paint and place them around the room in bowls after the party has been going for a while.

Some people are sure to try and eat them.

YUM!

Enjoy washing out a can of cat or dog food and replacing it with tuna or a similar food substance and walking out to a room full of people casually eating out of the can with a fork.

GOLF BALL MARSHMALLOWS

Buy a bag of jumbo-sized marshmallows from a grocery store. Head to the nearest golf course.

Follow the group of golfers ahead of you or take time so the party behind you will be very close.

Then, when the other people aren't looking, throw the marshmallows all over the green.

Having done that, the people will look for their balls, but it will be nearly impossible to find them from a distance with marshmallows all over the grass!

MAY I JOIN THE PARTY?

Next time you are at a park and there are families picnicking there, choose a big, extended family party and just sit amongst them as if you belong.

They won't really know whether you have come with another family member and so they probably won't say anything to you at first.

They may even share their picnic with you.

If they challenge you say, 'Oh, I came with Tom. He's gone to the toilet.'

See how long you can last.

RESTAURANT GUEST

When you go to a restaurant, give your name as Pupupu to the maitre-de.

When he calls you to your table you will hear, 'Pu-pu-pu Party of four'.

You can play the same joke but give your name as Connie Lingus, Dick Hertz, Harry Colon, etc.

WIZARD OF WHAT?

Rent porn tapes from the video store and record another film over them—like *Milo and Otis* or *Snow White* or *The Wizard of Oz*.

Just imagine the next person who gets them.

WHAT WAS THAT NOISE?

Make a pile of metal objects beside the telephone.

You could use pots and pans, metal folding chairs, saucepan lids.

Telephone a restaurant and ask to book a table.

Halfway through the conversation push the noisy pile over and say something like, 'No, no! Oh jeez. Oh . . .'

And fade off.

The person on the other end will think that something has happened to you and will try to get your attention.

Listen and enjoy the panic.

WHO? WHO?

This one is an oldie but a goodie:
Telephone a business and ask for Oscar.

If they reply that there is no Oscar at that address, say 'Thank you' and hang up.

Wait and then using another voice, ring the same number and ask to speak to Oscar.

When they tell you that Oscar doesn't work here, say 'Thank you', and hang up.

Do this several times during the following week.

At the end of the week, ring the number and say, 'This is Oscar. Has anyone called for me this week?'

HAPPY DAZE . . .

Spin and dance your way through a shopping centre singing a happy song to yourself.

TICK TOCK

Go to the local department store clock department.
Set all the clocks so that the alarms go off within minutes of each other.

Take a vantage point behind a rack of clothing and enjoy the fun while the poor sales person tries to find out which ones are going off!

HAVEN'T SEEN YOU FOR AGES!

Arrange with a few friends to 'accidentally' meet in a certain section of the department store.

Make a huge fuss.

'Oh, I haven't seen you for yonks! How is that brother of yours who was thrown into jail for forgery?'

Make up silly things, but be sure to say it in a loud voice so that everyone can hear.

GLUE FUN

At McDonald's, superglue a drink container and an empty packet to the tray.

Move to another table and watch and giggle as the assistant tries to empty the contents of the tray into the rubbish bin.

MY CHIPS!

McDonald's is a great place to simply bend over and take a French fry from somebody's meal as they are eating it.

This must be done with quick clean movements, so that the diner doesn't quite know whether he is having hallucinations or not.

PLAY HOG

Also at McDonald's, hog the play equipment and if challenged by a small child, simply hold your ground and refuse to move.

Say, 'I was here first.'

It will look pretty pathetic, a grown person sitting on the slide stopping the kids from playing.

If challenged by a mother, look sad and say, 'I'm going to tell my mother when she comes. I'm just as entitled to be here as anybody else.'

CATCHING UP ON THE NEWS

Walk into a furniture shop from the street.

Find a comfortable chair and sit down on it.

Take out the newspaper.

Read the paper and wait for the assistant to come up to you and ask if you need any help.

Tell him/her, 'No, I am quite comfortable, thank you.'

Continue reading your paper.

When you have finished, fold the paper, put it back in your bag, stand up, re-plump the cushions and move off.

STUCK SALT

Superglue the pepper and salt shakers to a café table.

They will be impossible to move when it comes to table wiping time.

THAY THAT AGAIN?

When ordering something from a shop, put on a lisp and get just one or two words wrong.

The patient shop assistant will try to understand what you are saying without embarrassing you.

After she/he is almost losing patience, take a deep breath and say your order perfectly.

Then exclaim, 'There I did it!' and clap.

RAVE PARTY

This is a great sight gag to play in a music store that has the earphones on the wall where you can listen individually to the latest hits.

Take a group of your coolest friends and visit the store.

Ask the shop assistant to play the grooviest dance music that you know of.

When the assistant has put the CD on, begin by listening quietly and then burst into dance.

Your friends will all do the same.

When the track finishes, calmly put down the earphones and thank the assistant.

Leave the store.

GOSH! WHAT A FAST ONE!

This is a joke that can be played at Saturday morning sports. It is best played on someone who boasts about what a good sportsperson they are.

The victim of the joke will probably end up getting their eyes checked.

You will have to organise this very well, as there is more than one person involved.

You will need three people to play this joke, so you will need to enlist the support of the catcher or wicketkeeper and also the umpire.

Agree on a secret signal that you can give when you, as pitcher or bowler, are going to play the joke.

Tell the umpire and the wicketkeeper about the secret signal so they know when the joke is going to take place.

You could also let other members of the team in on the joke so everyone can enjoy it.

This practical joke works well in a game of softball, rounders or cricket.

It could also be adapted to be used in a game of tennis.

Your victim thinks he is pretty crash-hot and goes in to bat.

The pitcher or bowler releases the ball.

The catcher or wicketkeeper yells and raises their hands.

They claim they've caught the ball after it hit the bat.

The victim did not even see the ball approach and is certain that it did not hit their bat. However, the umpire also says that the ball was caught after hitting the bat.

The umpire tells the victim that they are out.

In the spirit of fair play, the victim should be told about the joke shortly after they have left the field.

ART FARTY

This is a great joke to play if your school has an Annual Art Show. You will need to get the co-operation of one of the organisers for this to be successful.

The idea of this joke is to enter a picture that has no artistic merit at all and to get people discussing it.

Here are a few suggestions:

• An ink spot on white paper
• A piece of paper with a single piece of string hanging off it
• A piece of paper with two stripes painted on it

- A crumpled piece of paper glued to a piece of paper of a different colour.

  Give your work of art a title and write it on the label.

  The name should be as unusual as the artwork.

  Take your picture, label and some tape to an art show.

  Have it hung along with the other artworks.

  At the art show, start discussing your work of art with your friends loudly so that people can hear you.

  Before long, you'll have many people discussing your work.

PRANKS TO PLAY ON NEIGHBOURS

BALLOON'S UP!

You'll need some balloons and a balloon pump for this one. Insert the balloon, attached to the end of the balloon pump inside your neighbour's letterbox.

Then inflate the balloon and tie it off.

Your neighbour will be very confused as to how someone managed to get a fully inflated balloon through the letterbox!

EARLY MORNINGS

Alter a sign that advertises a car for sale or a garage sale so that it announces the time to be very early in the morning.

Your friend won't be able to figure out why people come around at half past five!

CARROT PATCH

Go to your local home and garden centre and load up on carrot seeds.

Then when the coast is clear, sprinkle the seeds on the lawn of your intended victim.

I always feel a smiley face beats spelling out something rude, but I'll leave it to you to decide how mean you want to be.

At first nothing will happen.

The seeds need to germinate.

Then come springtime or if it is summertime, a few weeks after sprinkling, the seeds will start to grow.

The carrots are a different shade of green than the grass and they have a different shape of leaf so they really stand out.

The best thing is that you cannot sprinkle weed killer on the carrots because the only weed killers that work on a lawn are for broad leaf plants and carrots are narrow leaf.

The only way to get rid of them is to pick them one by one.

GARAGE SALE

Take out an ad in your local paper advertising an 'Estate Sale: Antiques! Starting at 6 am.'

Then just before dawn on the day of the 'sale', put some Estate Sale signs on the ends of the street where your victim lives and on their front fence.

People usually start showing up about an hour early for those things and people will keep coming by all morning!

It's best to do it on a weekend when the victim planned to sleep in.

WHERE'S THE CAR

If you're with your friend in a parking lot and they run in the store to pick something up and leave you in the car, move it to a different spot, so when they come out it's not there. Watch the look on their face . . . it's priceless!

BODY ON THE SIDE WALK

This is a great prank to play on your mates if you happen to live in an apartment building.

Knock on your neighbour's door.

Say in supposed panic, 'I've got to use your window, someone's about to jump from an apartment above yours.'

Run to window and look outside, but don't let the victim look.

At this point your accomplice dumps a rag-filled dummy either from the window above or from the roof.

The dummy should be fully clothed.

For added realism, put some plastic bags of fake blood inside the clothes.

On the sidewalk below, a third accomplice puts down a plastic sheet, then covers it with a sheet painted to resemble the sidewalk.

After the body hits, let the victim see the gore, then convince him to run down and help while you stay and call the ambulance.

As soon as the victim has left, signal your accomplice to remove the sheets and the dummy and head for some prearranged hiding place.

Then you leave the apartment and disappear somewhere in the building; later, you make your way downstairs and leave.

The victim will race downstairs expecting to find a dead bloody body and will instead see only clean, empty pavement.

Of course, it is best done late at night since the joke would be spoiled by a passer-by who informed the victim of the body's fate.

The fun comes imagining the victim trying to convince the police or anyone else of what happened!

MY CAR IS BETTER THAN YOUR CAR!

This practical joke is good for a young man who is in love with his car and wants to continually tell you how good it is.

This joke is made funny by the fact that anything that his car does that is good, will most surely be related in glowing terms to his family and friends.

Unbeknown to him, add four litres of petrol each night into the victim's fuel tank.

Repeat the exercise every day for about ten days to two weeks.

You can be sure that he will tell everyone what great performance he is getting out of his car.

Wait for his story each day to get better and better.

Then, each night for two weeks, remove four litres of fuel from the victim's tank.

Will he be quite as vocal about the poor performance of his car as he was about the excellent mileage he achieved in the recent past?

You may choose to tell him or you may just let him wonder.

UNLOCKED CAR

If you know that a friend or neighbour regularly leaves his/her car unlocked, this is a fun trick to play.

Open the car and turn on everything—turn up the radio, turn on the windshield wipers, the blinkers and anything else that might confuse them.

Sit back and watch.

WELCOME

Get yourself some balsa-wood (usually found at hobby shops) and make yourself a fake mallet handle and head.

Paint the head black and the handle dark brown, so that it looks like a real, lethal, sledgehammer.

When company comes to visit, throw it at them when they walk in the door.

The utter shock and expressions on their faces are priceless.

FEATHER FLYING!

If you have a friend or neighbour with a ride-on lawnmower this is a fun prank to play.

When your friend is absent, take a plastic bag full of feathers and old hamburger meat, thawed and cut into tiny pieces.

Take some scotch tape and tape the bag of feathers and meat securely to the bottom of the lawn mower in front of the blade.

When your friend starts mowing, the vibrating will slowly shake the bag loose and then, 'fur' and 'guts' will fly everywhere!

This is especially good if your friend has a small dog or pet.

MESSAGE ON THE LAWN

Do you have a neighbour who makes life difficult for everyone by constantly complaining about everything and everyone in the neighbourhood?

Does he/she take the kid's balls when they go over the fence and refuse to return them; does he/she threaten to poison the dog if it barks again; does he/she take to the cat with a hose if it wanders on his/her turf?

Here's a way to get back and to continue getting back for a while to come.

Buy a packet of Lawn Food and write him/her a message on the front lawn.

Tell him/her what you really think.

No doubt he/she will see it—the letters will stand out—and become angry.

But his/her first instinct will be to hose those unwanted sentiments right away.

Of course, by washing the words away with her hose, he/she will be unwittingly adding to the trick by providing the moisture for the Lawn Food to do its work.

The grass will be greener and lusher in those places where the lawn food has been watered in and the wording on the lawn will last for two or three seasons for the entire world to read.

FOR NEIGHBOURS WHO ARE HARD TO GET ON WITH:

Got a neighbour that's a real pain in the ass?

Do they have a lawn?

Do they have a garden that's accessible?

Yes to all the above?

Great!

Go out and get yourself some grass-killer and fill the sucker's hose with the stuff.

Then sit back and wait for them to water their lawn!

A RIGHT PLONKER

Does the person that you want to get even with drink red wine?

If so, have I got one for you!

Get yourself some Neutral Red, a water soluble, crystalline, red dye.

Mix some into the person's wine and wait for them to take a leak.

Neutral Red comes out as red as it goes in and people have a tendency to get really nervous when they start pissing what they think is blood!

ON THE NOSE

This one takes a bit of time for preparation, so it's not too good for spontaneous revenge.

But it's worth the time!

Get a quart jar with a rubber seal.

Pour about one cm of crystal Drano along with about 3 cm or so, of warm water into the jar.

Place the lid on the jar and allow the mixture to sit in a warm place for about an hour.

Take the lid off and add six egg whites (no yokes).

Add a quarter cup of Methylene Blue and then fill the jar to within a couple of centimetres of the top with water.

Seal the jar tightly and allow to sit for four to six weeks.

When the 'bomb' is ready to use, you can either throw it like a Molotov cocktail or shake it up and pour the contents out.

Avoid getting any over yourself as you will smell for a week.

The results have to be smelled, to be believed!

DEAD DOG

This can be good, but requires a certain amount of cold blooded resolve and lack of personal attachment to the dead animal that you are using.

Nobody is suggesting for a minute that you go out and kill anything, but you could utilise some piece of road kill that you come across for the joke.

Go to a pet shop and buy a fancy looking pet collar and leash.

Identify the person that you wish to play the prank upon.

Take the road kill to which you have attached the collar and leash and tie that to the rear bumper of the car belonging to your victim.

Make sure to toss dead animal under the car so it won't be seen.

When your victim drives away, chances are he/she will be stopped by either a cop or a member of some animal lovers group for dragging some poor defenceless pet down the road.

Either way, they are gonna have some awful quick explaining to do!

SLOW DOWN, THERE'S A COP CAR

If you or your friend has a car that looks like an undercover police car, this is a good prank to play on other road users and may have the added benefit of slowing traffic down a bit.

It is excellent if you can pick up an old police hat or one that looks like one and just place it on the back seat rest of the car so that it can be seen through the back window.

Usually this prank operates more effectively if you have two people in the car in dark clothes that might be mistaken for policemen.

Then take the car cruising.

Watch other motorist's reactions when they see you out of the corner of your eye and think that you're a cop and that you may nab them.

People will be reluctant to pass you if you are sitting on the speed limit.

Others will come speeding up behind you, spot you, slow down and then accelerate again when they realise that you are not a threat.

Great fun!

SNOW BUSINESS

If you have a neighbour that you do not get on with and if you live in an area where it snows, then here is an easy prank to play.

Take a snow shovel.

Shovel all the snow out of your yard, into his driveway.

He might have a little trouble pulling out of his driveway the next day.

MAIL ORDERS

Send in subscriptions to embarrassing magazines in the victim's name.

Make sure to check 'Bill Me'.

MORE MAIL

Send off a request in the victim's name to numerous foreign postage stamp bureaus requesting ordering information, to be put on mailing lists, etc. The response is quite astounding.

SAY WHERE?

Get change of address cards from the post office and change the victim's address to someplace like Guam.

SPEED TRAP

At lunch time, sit in a parked car facing the street.
Wear dark sunglasses and aim a blow dryer at passing cars.

Watch the neighbours slow down thinking you're a cop.

They'll fall for it every time.

PRECIOUS NEW CAR

This one is great to do on people who have new cars or are really protective of their cars.

Find their car in a parking lot and write a note that says something like sorry about the scratch, here's my number.

Naturally you don't put your real number.

Watch your victim as they come to their car and read the note; watch them try to find a scratch on their car.

Some will spend ages looking over every bit of the panels.

PRACTICAL JOKES TO PLAY ON THE FAMILY

COLOURED PLANT

You can add food colouring to the soil of a potted plant for some rather weird pigmentation.

TASTE THAT!

Bicarbonate of soda is a fabulous cooking ingredient. Many don't realise its powerful pranking possibilities.

Bicarbonate of soda tastes disgusting, but can be easily mistaken for sherbet, flour, caster sugar, etc.

Also try rolling bonbons in it and handing them to a friend!

SHOWER OF LOVE

This is a joke to play on a member of your family who is studying and who regularly uses a desk.

You will need time to set this joke up as it is quite complicated.

Run a string from the drawer of the desk, up the wall, into the ceiling and to a spot directly over where your victim will sit.

When the subject sits at a desk and when he/she pulls out a drawer a string runs from the back of the drawer, up the wall, into the ceiling, over to a spot directly over the subject's head.

It triggers the trap, whose action snaps a card away from its position covering a funnel, releasing a handful of glitter, which flows down the funnel, through its spout and onto the subject.

It is wonderful to watch.

You will hear a muffled snapping noise, a quiet 'chuff', and watch the slow, glittery descent of a cloud of brightly coloured dust settle over the head and shoulders of your subject.

LOTTERY WINNER

If you have a local lottery where you get to pick your own numbers, buy a fresh newspaper with last night's winning numbers, then buy a ticket with those very same numbers.

Gleefully announce that you have the numbers.

Your family will carefully check the numbers against each other.

It may take them quite a while to realise that you have the numbers in the next draw.

BIRTHDAY SURPRISE

While wrapping someone's birthday or Christmas present, fill the wrapping paper with tiny foam balls and the circles from a hole-punch.

When the intended recipient opens the parcel the paper and foam will fall out everywhere and really surprise them!

IS THAT THE TIME?

Gather up a lot of alarm clocks and set them to go off at various times throughout the night.

Then simply place them under your intended victim's bed for a memorable night.

It is also possible, if your victim is a heavy sleeper, to put the clocks in a metal bucket, which will increase the intensity of the sound.

SCRAMBLED PICS

Take a transceiver like the ones ham radio operators use—3 watts or more is good—and push 'Transmit' while near the TV at home. This will have the effect of semi-scrambling whatever is showing.

The more powerful the transceiver, the more the TV signal gets messed up.

This does work on cable TV, too.

Watch as Dad, especially, tries to fix the picture.

GOO

Leave toothpaste on the underside of light switches and doorknobs.

TIME BOMB

Use appliance timers to detonate stereo equipment at high volume.

WHAT ARE WE EATING?

Carefully remove the labels from some tins of food and reglue them on different tins. Have a look at Mum's face when she opens a can of 'beans' and finds that it is spaghetti.

IKEA FURNITURE

Leave someone's furniture in a 99% disassembled state. Repeat as necessary.

BISCUITS IN BED

Break up a biscuit over your victim's bed into tiny crumbs and cover it with the bed sheets—it takes ages to clear!

STICKY PHONE

Coat the receiver of the phone with shoe polish and then wait for a call.

Small amounts of shaving cream work too.

STUCK

Glue the telephone receiver down and then organise somebody to make lots of calls.

CHARITY

Make pledges to charities in a family member's name. Be generous.

CAREFUL NOW

Tell your family member about a neat magic trick you just learned how to perform. Get a glass of water and tell him to place both his hands flat on the table with his palms down.

Now, tell him to put one hand on top of the other.

Place the cup of water on top of his hands and walk away.

If he moves, they will get water over them.

This can also be done by telling him to kneel down like a table and placing the glass on his back.

SALTY SURPRISE

When making sugar cookies, omit the sugar and replace with salt. It is a good idea to make the real thing using the real recipe for a few times to get people used to how wonderful your cookies are.

Then substitute the salt for the sugar.

Indicate that you have changed the recipe slightly—to cut down on your sugar intake—but that you think they taste just as good, if not better!

CONFETTI DAY

Fill someone's umbrella with confetti, wait until a rainy day and enjoy.

DON'T STEP IN IT

Put doggie do in a paper bag, light the bag with a match, put on someone's doorstep.

Ring the bell and watch them stamp it out.

GIBBERISH

Crack open someone's audio cassettes and flip the tape over so that what comes out is pure gibberish.

BURNING SENSATION

Hold a magnifying glass over someone in your family who is sunbathing out by the pool.

Be prepared to run shortly after you do this.

STRONG COFFEE

Put pure crystallised caffeine in someone's coffee pot. This will make espresso seem like milk.

FUNNY, RUNNY

Bake brownies or cookies and substitute Ex-Lax for part of the chocolate.

Use some chocolate to keep the taste right.

ASSA(U)LTED

Rig the lid of salt shakers to fail when used, resulting in a veritable salt lick on the victim's food.

STICKY BUM

Place Vaseline or some other reasonably clear gel, on the dunny seat at night.

Listen for the screams.

SHAMPISS

Urinate in a person's shampoo.

HAIR TODAY, GONE TOMORROW

Put Nair or some other hair removal chemical in a person's shampoo or conditioner. You may need to distract the person for a moment to let the stuff take a better hold.

STICKY SHOWER

Unscrew the shower head and place three or four lifesaver lollies in it.

Re-screw it.

Lifesavers are great since they dissolve and then reform on the victim.

The victim will feel sticky afterwards and of course the solution to that is to take another shower . . .

HOT AND COLD

Flush toilets while a person showers.

The more toilets, the better.

HARD TO GET AT

Glue the lids to people's shampoo shut.

They get all wet and then realise they can't wash their hair.

CIGARETTE SMOKERS

If you have a smoker in the family, do him/her a favour.

In a soft pack of cigarettes, carefully cut the bottom cellophane and proceed to open the pack carefully from the bottom.

Remove three or more cigarettes—always less than five as this will become noticeable—and glue the pack back up with clear-drying glue.

Re-seal the pack.

Stand back and watch as the victim realises they have just purchased a 'new' pack with less than 20 cigarettes.

PARTY TRICK

If you are having a party at your own house get about five wine glasses and put cling film in each—dip it in so it is only about half way in.

Now lay them out on the table with a wine bottle.

Dim the lights so the guests won't see you have jinxed their glass.

Tell them to help themselves to the wine.

They will pour wine into their glass and eventually realise it is only half full.

This is very effective.

HIDDEN PHONE

While at a party or at someone's house or apartment, remove all of the phone cables when no one is looking but leave an answering machine (preferably hidden).

That way when the phone rings the machine will pick up and the resident will be unable to talk.

It's very confusing and annoying.

SNAKES ALIVE!

Buy a rubber snake and use fishing line to tie around its head. Tape it to the lid of the toilet.

When target gets home, she will go into the bathroom, lift the toilet lid and scream bloody murder when the snake comes out of the water to 'attack' her!

WET MISTAKE

Don't want someone to come into your room? Get a large plastic cup, fill it with water and set it carefully on the top of a partially opened door.

Post a warning sign on the door that reads, 'Do Not Open!'

When they inevitably do open the door, the cup will fall, dousing them with water.

MESSY!

Simply sprinkle birdseed on the roof of your brother's much loved new car.

Bird droppings are rather difficult to remove!

WORM IN THE APPLE

Trick the children by cutting a hole in their lunch time apple and inserting a gummy worm in it.

WHAT TIME IS IT?

There's a major drawback to this trick in that the perpetrator suffers along with everybody else, but early risers should find it's worth the lost sleep.

Get the children up for school.

Get yourself all ready for work.

When breakfast is over, open the curtains and when you do the family will see a sign that says, 'It's 3am—April Fool!'

COLOURED MILK

If your family likes a nice bowl of cold cereal with milk for breakfast give them milk that has been dyed green and tell them that the cows have eaten too much grass.

TASTES DIFFERENT

Take some Oreo cookies.
Undo the tops, one at a time and place a small circle of wax paper in between the cookie and the filling.

Then set them out to watch your victim take a big bite!

ALIEN INVASION

Take a mini-tape recorder and record the words 'They're coming for you.'

Turn volume setting to whisper and press play as your family member sleeps.

Hide somewhere inconspicuous.

JUST NOT COOL

Insert an extremely cheesy CD (preferably Barry Manilow) into a cool family member's favourite CD case.

Make sure that the CDs look similar.

After they unwittingly put the CD in without checking, watch their expressions as the room is filled with 'Copacabana'.

Continue to switch CDs as needed.

HOPPY

Staple the cuffs of a male family member's pants together and watch them hop.

MOUTH WASH

Like someone to have really clean teeth?
Give them a tube of toothpaste.

But only after you've opened the tube of toothpaste and held it tightly together with an opened tube of shaving cream and squeezed some of the shaving cream into the toothpaste.

JOKES TO PLAY ON LITTLE KIDS

WHAT'S THAT, FROG?

Suggest to a small child that if they drink too much green cordial they will turn into a frog.

When he/she tries to protest that that won't happen say to him/her, 'Sorry, you'll have to croak more clearly as I can't understand you.'

When he/she protests even more say, 'Hop over here and tell me!'

You can take this joke on and get an hour or two of fun from it.

HOT RED!

You could try the same with red cordial, by telling your small child that if he/she drinks too much red cordial he/she will turn bright red.

Then touch his/her cheek and make a sizzle noise.

Make a noise like the smoke alarm and pretend to call the fire brigade.

If you are outside get a bucket of water and chase to try and cool him/her down.

You could also chase him/her with the hose.

BLUE, BLUE, BLUE

Suggest that if a child drinks blue juice or cordial that he/she will turn into a Smurf.

Wait until the little one goes to sleep and take a blue marker and colour the tip of his/her nose and the ears.

Wait for the fun in the morning.

APE SHOW

Use an ape mask and speak in a long slow voice or sing the song 'I am the Apeman and have come to get you'.

Keep up the act all afternoon and enjoy the reaction.

GORILLA IN HIDING

Make a sign saying, 'Beware of the Gorilla' and using the same disguise as above, hide behind a dense bush.

When a small child comes near, jump up and make ape noises and chase them, just letting them run fast enough to avoid capture.

WATER GORILLA

Hide in the bush and when someone reads the sign jump out and throw water bombs, making sure that you just miss the mark.

WHAT IS THAT BLUE MARK ON YOUR FOREHEAD?

Fill in one side of a coin with the felt pen or cover it with powder. Make-up powder is very good for this purpose.

Stand in front of your victim and press the coin that is not marked onto your forehead.

When your victim asks what you are doing, tell them that you heard on the radio that people who can stick coins to their forehead are supposed to be smarter than those who can't.

Your victim will probably want to have a go, so that they can prove how smart they are.

Tell the victim that you'll show them exactly where the coin has to go.

Take the coin that has the marked side and press that side firmly in the middle of the victim's forehead.

Make sure the victim does not see the marks or powder.

Tell the victim to hold the coin firmly in place for two minutes.

After two minutes, tell the victim to let go.

If the coin is stuck to the forehead, pull the coin off and tell them that they are obviously very intelligent.

If the coin falls off, grab it and put it in your pocket.

Tell them that you couldn't make the coin stick either.

This will make them feel better.

Whether the coin sticks or falls, the victim will have an impression of the coin stuck on their forehead and they will walk around without realising it.

SPECIAL TOPPING

Get some vanilla ice cream.

Put several scoops of it into a nice ice cream dish.

Then, just like you are preparing a chocolate sundae, spoon on the topping.

But, instead of chocolate, use Vegemite.

CUTLERY

Every time you go to your victim's house, put a couple of plastic forks, spoons, whatever in the silverware drawer.

Pretty soon they will empty it out and begin to think they are nuts.

DISAPPEARING DRINK

Before doing this trick, hide a drinking straw in your pocket. Tell everyone that your can make a drink disappear—completely, without touching it!

Fill up a plastic cup with water and blindfold one of the children while you put the cup on his friend's head.

Then take the drinking straw out of your pocket and drink the contents of the cup—making sure you do not touch the sides of the cup.

The drink has now disappeared!

YUK!

Take a sherbet, empty the contents into a bowl for later consumption.

Then fill the packet with a mixture of salt and sugar and hand it to a friend!

A SHOWER OF CONFETTI

Place confetti on top of a fan and ask someone to turn the fan on. Try also using hole-punch leftovers or chalk dust.

RAIN DROPS

Fill an umbrella that the kids use with hole-punch waste or talc. Create a sudden shower when opened!

CAUGHT YOU!

Tell your child about a neat magic trick you just learned how to perform.

Get a glass of water and tell the child to place both his hands flat on the table with his palms down.

Now, tell him to put one hand on top of the other.

Place the cup of water on top of his hands and walk away.

If the child moves he will get water over them.

This can also be done by telling him to kneel down like a table and placing the glass on his back.

WHAT'S THE TIME?

When you spot your little person carrying something in their hands, simply ask them what the time is!

JASS, HUGH . . .

Dial a regular phone number.

Say, 'May I speak to a man with the last name of Jass and the first name of Hugh. He uses the restroom a lot. Ask for someone to search for Hugh Jass in the bathroom.'

IS THE KING THERE?

Call up someone in the phone book named Presley and ask to speak to Elvis.

Be very forceful, insist that you have the correct number.

If they ask if this is a prank phone call, just sing 'You Ain't Nothin' but a Hound Dog' and then hang up.

A SORRY TALE

Call any number.

Ask if it is Bud's Auto Repairs.

When the person says, 'No', say, 'Well, can I talk to you because this is really bothering me.'

Tell him/her that you just picked up your car from this Bud's Auto Repairs.

Continue by telling a long-winded story, something like, 'My little boy Clinton really wanted to go to the park, so I just had to, 'cause he did the little puppy dog look and that just breaks my heart, so I took him and he kept complaining about gross things, but he always makes up silly things, because he is a silly boy. I looked at him in the rear view mirror and he was pointing, so I looked to where he was pointing and there was a piece of poopy in the seat beside him. This disgusted me and I think my son is really scared from this experience. No one should have to go through something like that. Don't you think?'

Then thank them for listening and hang up.

GIBBONS FOR SALE

Telephone people by the name of Gibbon.
Tell them that you are from the zoo and that you wish to buy two gibbons.

Ask have they any for sale.

LIBRARY FINES

Telephone a number. And leave a message that you are from the library and that the book fines totalling $156.17 are long overdue and must be paid immediately to avoid affecting the person's credit rating.

A CONVERSATION THAT YOU COULD HAVE WITH A CONVENIENCE STORE

Hello, is this 7 Eleven?
I have a few questions for you.

I was wondering if you guys have security cameras.

I was down there last week and I stole a shit load of stuff and I wanted to know if I'd get caught on the video.

I got a couple of bottles of coke, a snickers bar and a hot dog.

My name's not important . . . What I want to know is how long you keep those tapes and if I'm busted.

Well, can you tell me if there's a security guard down there at the moment?

Well, is there one or not?

Okay then. Do you guys have a gun on the premises?

I want to know if I should pack heat or whether I should just bring my Crocodile Dundee knife with me.

So have you got a knife down there? I think that might be illegal . . . maybe I should call the police and report your store.

CHILD ON THE LINE

Phone any number that you can order things from (such as a home shopping network, etc).

When the phone is answered, start ordering the item and speak in a voice that is neither a man's voice nor a lady's voice.

Say that your name is Pat or Billy or Sam or any unisex name.

The confused operator will try to establish your sex without being rude.

Ask weird questions like, 'Okay, so is this 14 carat pair of gold earrings made with wool?' or 'Is this lighter flame resistant?'

Towards the end of the conversation and while you are in the middle of a sentence have your friend yell into the phone in a shrill mother's voice, 'DARCY! DARCY! WHAT THE HELL! ARE YOU CALLIN' THOSE PORN SITES AGAIN? GET BACK HERE YOU LITTLE BASTARD!'

Make a noise like you dropped the phone and pull the phone about a metre from your mouth so it sounds like you're in the background and start slapping your hands together and making all of this noise and have your friend start crying like a little kid and so it sounds like your beating your child!

DIAL WHO?

Reprogram the speed calling on the family telephone so that instead of getting Dad at the office, you get dial-a-joke, instead of getting Grandma you get dial-a-joke, etc.

RUSSIAN ROULETTE

Call up a vet, using a strong Russian accent.
Ask how much it will cost to have your son neutered.

When you get an answer of disbelief, insist that back in Russia, the local horse doctor neutered you when you were 12 years old.

BARKING MAD

Telephone a friend and when they answer the telephone simply bark like a dog.

Bark like a dog in reply to everything that they say.

Keep it going as long as you can.

Lots of fun.

WAKE UP!

When you are up late, telephone a friend.
This will wake him/her up.
Say,
'Wakey, wakey. Time for eggs and bakey.'
He/she will not be happy.

NAUGHTY DOROTHY!

Telephone the video store and say how upset you are that
somebody had switched the copy of *The Wizard of Oz* with the
video *Naughty Bedroom Capers* and that the couple whose little girl
saw 15 minutes of it before the parents realised are suing.

PERSONAL QUESTIONS

A good trick to play is to telephone a few of your friends and to tell
them that you are from the school and that you are doing a survey
of the whole of your year level on health and human development.

Ask whether they would take the time to answer a few questions
over the phone.

Proceed to ask embarrassing questions about their personal life
and their boyfriends.

Great for a laugh.

CHEAP DIVE

Call up a local skydiving centre and ask if it is possible to book a
family dive.

Ask will it be any cheaper if 'we all go on the same parachute'.

BE QUIET!

Ring a fundraising telethon and offer to make a donation if they get it off the air.

ANY MESSAGES FOR ME?

Get a number of friends to assemble at a place with a telephone. Use either going to a telephone booth or a phone that you do not own, in case the victim has caller ID.

One at a time, call the victim and ask for a person named Jeremy or any other name of your choice.

After the third caller has called, the victim is bound to become really annoyed.

After all ten have called, you call him and say, 'Hello, would you please tell me if anyone left a message for me on your phone? My name is Jeremy and I was expecting some really important calls, but couldn't attend to them due to some important work. Thanks!'

Listen to whatever the victim says, laugh together and hang up.

This is a classic prank and can work on almost any gathering.

SARS VICTIM

Dial a random number.

When it is picked up say, 'We regret to inform you but, due to SARS, people as ugly as you must be quarantined for five years. Please report immediately to your local doctor.'

Then hang up.

PRACTICAL JOKES
USING PLUMBER'S TAPE

THERE'S A CUP ON YOUR CAR!

Secure a cup to the top of your car with duct tape on the bottom of the cup.

As if you had left it there by mistake, drive merrily along with the radio loud so that you can't hear the people yelling to get your drink off the car.

When they point and wave, act like they are waving at you, smile and wave back.

You would not believe the reactions to this in traffic.

People will even get out of their vehicle and tap on the window to tell you about the cup!

BLOCKED DOORWAY

This is a classic!
Duct tape plastic wrap in the doorway of a very dimly lit room and wait for some unsuspecting victim to enter the room.

TOILET PAPER SHOE

Take a two metre piece of toilet paper and attach a piece of duct tape to one end (half of the tape on the toilet paper, half hanging off the roll).

Place the paper and the tape—sticky-side-up—on the floor at the entrance of the bathroom.

When your victim steps on the tape, they will be dragging the toilet paper from their shoe.

THIEF

Sometimes when you buy used videos from the video store, they still have the little anti-theft strip on them.

So if you ever want to get someone good, just remove theft strip and duct tape it to the bottom of their shoe, then send him on a run to the video store.

Works great!

TYRE TROUBLE

Get some bubble wrap with 2 cm bubbles (at most office supply stores or in dumpsters behind gift shops).

Cut a strip about 50 cm long and the width of a tyre.

Tape this to the tread of the front wheel of a parked car.

When the car starts moving, the resultant popping sounds like a machine gun.

A MARKED MAN

Before leaving the office one night, take a small strip of black duct tape and tape the sink sprayer handle in the 'on' position and aim the sprayer so it will hit the boss square in the chest.

Watch for the water mark next day.

STUCK DRAWER

A few feet of plumber tape taped to someone's centre desk drawer will shut it around the edges of the two sides and the back.

It's doubly exciting if the drawer is just slightly open, so that the victim can tell that the drawer can't be locked, but can't immediately see or feel what is holding the drawer shut if the tape doesn't cover the entire length of the drawer.

At the same time it doesn't do any permanent damage to the furniture.

This works best in conditions of reduced light.

Avoid doing this to anyone who may have a bad back.

The drawer pulling response can get really vigorous.

LONG NIGHT

When out camping with your mates, duct tape one of the party to his bed.

He will not be able to get out of bed in the morning.

CONDIMENT SURPRISE

Take a ketchup packet, honey packet, mustard packet or any other individually packeted potential squirting mess and fold it.

Then duct tape it on the rim under the pad that separates the toilet seat from the toilet. When your potential subject sits down on the seat—they will receive a condiment surprise.

BIG BANG

Use duct tape to rig those 'booby trap' firecrackers, with the strings coming out of both ends.

For instance, duct tape one end to the toilet seat lid and the other to the seat.

When the lid is lifted—BANG!

CONSTANT RING

Sneak up to someone's house in the middle of the night and duct tape their doorbell down.

SHOWER ANYBODY?

You will need:
Duct tape, plastic bag, shower head and victim.

You have to stay up late and make sure you don't wake up your victim.

Take the plastic bag and tape it around the shower head, making sure it is on tight.

Then just wait for the unsuspecting person to try to take a shower.

NO MOUSE

Put a strip of duct tape over the mouse ball or optical sensor on a computer mouse. When your colleague tries to use the mouse, it won't work.

SENSIBLE

Go to one of those bathrooms that have sensor toilets and put a peace of duct tape over the sensor so that the toilet never flushes or put it over the sensor on the sink so the water is always on.

CAR JOB

Gather a lot of cling wrap and a lot of duct tape, remembering that if you spare the duct tape you spare the job or prank.

Next, wrap your victim's car in the cling wrap, making sure that you don't apply the tape directly to paint.

If you do it properly you will wrap the car in a sort of duct tape cocoon.

Sit back and watch your victim open his package.

SINKING CHAIRS

Here is a fun and safe prank to pull on co-workers in an office setting.

Most office dwellers have chairs that use a pneumatic piston to control the height.

They are also designed to use a person's weight to effect the downward adjustment. While your co-workers are away from their desk, take a strip of duct tape and tape the height adjusting lever to the bottom of the seat.

This effectively locks the piston into adjust mode.

When they sit down, their weight will cause the chair to bottom out quickly.

The looks of utter confusion are priceless.

PRANKS TO PLAY IN CARS

NO HEAD INJURIES

Wear a motorcycle helmet while driving your car!
The looks you get from other drivers are fantastic.

You may also want to don a gas mask to heighten the effect.

You can tell curious drivers at the lights that the gas mask is for allergies and the helmet for extra protection in case the airbag accidentally inflates.

SLEEPING

While driving, wait until a car is slowly passing on the left, then lean your head back on the seat (or resting on the window) and close your left eye and let your mouth hang open like you're sleeping.

A little drool adds to the effect.

(Be sure to keep your right eye open to watch the road.)

DRIVE SINGER

Get a PA system or megaphone and sing while driving along.

A KIND ACT

Stop and pray for road kill.
Perhaps even erecting a little cross at the side of the road.

MEEEOOWW!

Keep at least five cats in the car.

BURNING ENGINE

Take motor oil or cooking oil and pour a small amount onto the engine of friend's/foe's car.

Make sure it is just a thin coat so as to not start a fire.

When the victim gets a couple of miles down the road and their car begins smoking profusely, they will assume the worst.

WHAT THE?

When you are going through a drive-thru, pretend that your car window is broken and order with the door open.

Close the door and open the window to receive the order!

PRANKS FOR UNIVERSITY STUDENTS TO PLAY

WHO PUT THAT THERE?

Find out when your lecturer is making photocopies of a document.

If the lecturer leaves the room or is distracted, now is the time to act.

Put a piece of clear tape on the glass window of the photocopier with a secret message, an embarrassing image or an insult to a member of staff.

The lecture notes will be far more interesting.

WRONG WORD

This can be applied to computers that are used by students in the library.

Alter the settings in Microsoft AutoCorrect so that whenever your victim types a specific word, it is replaced with something more comical.

WHAT A DIN!

For a large lecture auditorium, this will cause diversions for an hour or so.

Gather up a lot of alarm clocks and set them to go off at various times throughout the lecture.

Then simply place them under the seats in various places that won't be noticed.

Having some of the clocks in metal buckets will increase the intensity of the sound.

WHERE IS NUMBER 3?

Get three animals, sheep or pigs and number them: 1, 2 and 4. Set them loose in your local school or office.

People will spend forever trying to find the 'missing' one, number 3!

NB: Not really a good prank to do—think about the welfare of the animals.

HEARING VOICES

Record yourself and several friends making different sorts of bizarre comments and sounds on a tape in low, husky voices.

Place the tape recorder on top of a cupboard and invite another unsuspecting friend around.

Before they arrive start the tape playing on low volume.

When your friend queries the voices that they are hearing, act like you can't hear them and try to convince your friend that they're going mad.

Works a treat . . .

WHERE DID THEY COME FROM?

Release large numbers of pigeons into a gymnasium or lecture hall. (Young pigs in the hallway are good too.)

SQUIRT!

This is good to do in the canteen or at the footy where you have to serve yourself tomato sauce.

Take the top off a bottle of ketchup and put some bicarbonate of soda in.

Quickly screw the top back on and shake.

When someone opens the bottle the ketchup will squirt out—extremely messy!

CHICKEN IN THE CEILING

Release a chicken or similar noisy relatively light animal between a dropped ceiling (the ones with the tiles) and the actual ceiling.

They are tough enough to catch on normal ground!

NOW WHERE WERE WE?

When a teacher leaves the room, have everyone turn every desk and chair upside down.

When the teacher returns be sitting on your chairs working as if nothing had happened.

A TASTY MORSEL

When dissecting animals, take the liver (or some other brown organ), and place it in the instructor's coffee.

Place parts from your dissection in various places around a cafeteria salad bar.

PLENTY OF SEATING

Put every single chair from a large building in one room. The smaller the room the better.

Also good near the entrance to a building.

LUNCHTIME ENTERTAINMENT

Hire a stripper to appear in a high traffic area, such as a cafeteria during peak hours.

VENDING MACHINES

Fill several vending machines in a high traffic area with condoms and beer cans.

PUBLIC TRANSPORT

When on a bus, be as obnoxious as possible while loudly speaking another language (German, French, Spanish, etc.).

When you hear someone mutter something like, 'I wish they would shut up,' respond appropriately in perfect English.

POLITICAL RALLY

Start quasi-political parties at university for the sole purpose of being obnoxious, even though you don't really have anything meaningful to say.

Make emblems and post them on everything in sight, march around spewing meaningless propaganda.

You will be amazed at how many punters join the movement, especially if you have drinks after your meetings.

STONES THROW

Throw those fake foam rocks, which are available at novelty stores, at someone.

Works best when around real rocks such as in a geology class or outdoors.

DIVERTED

Get some cones or barrels and divert traffic from a nearby street through the campus.

POSITION VACANT

Advertise your Senior Lecturer's job in the local paper.

DUSTY

Place flour on top of the blades of the ceiling fans.
It might be days, even weeks, but one day, they will get turned on . . .

PENIS ENVY

Erect a large papier-mâché penis in a very public place.
Write messages on it for added effect.

CONGRATULATIONS

Hand the principal/headmaster some small item when getting your diploma. (Marbles, balloons, condoms, coins etc.)
Works best if everyone does it.

HOT STUDY

Attach a remote control to the fire alarm in a room and set it off from a safe distance. Watch the panic. When the panic subsides, do it again.
And again.
And . . . well you get the picture.

STUCK

Freeze glasses to trays in the cafeteria.
This can be accomplished by smearing the bottom of the glass with honey and sticking it firmly to the tray.
Next, fill the glass with ice, water and salt to lower the temperature.
After a few minutes the honey should be frozen to both the tray and the glass.

THIS IS A GREAT ONE FOR A PARTY!

Take your video camera (take someone else's, if you don't have one).

Enter your toilet room.

From the other side of the room to the toilet, stand on a chair and film a shot from near the ceiling of your toilet seat (about five minutes should do).

When someone leaves the room to visit the toilet, put the cassette in your video player.

Just before the person re-enters the room start playing the tape.

Ask everyone in the room to laugh at the TV screen.

Watch the face of the person re-entering the room!

BARGAIN

Print off a large 'FOR SALE' sign and put it in your mate's car window with his mobile/telephone number on it.

Make sure the price is ridiculously cheap—loads of fun!

COMPUTER PRANK

Some computer monitors have a cable with five BNC connectors at the monitor end—black, white, red, green and blue.

It's fun to mess with these—like switching the red, green and blue cables around for interesting colour effects: each cable carries the individual colour components that form the actual picture on the screen.

You can substitute red for green, green for blue and blue for red, if you like.

Don't touch the black and white cables, though.

Warning: Monitors are high voltage devices and are as such potentially dangerous: always power-down and unplug your monitor first.

POP GOES THE WEASEL

Place a couple of pieces of popcorn at the end of the tailpipe of your friend's car.

When they start to drive and it heats up, the popcorn starts popping.

Things will start getting a bit agitated in the driver's seat!

NB: Don't put enough in to block or restrict the air flow in the tailpipe—this would be very dangerous.

COLLAPSING CABINET

Remove the screws that hold filing cabinet handles on and then stick them back with blue tack.

Watch the surprise on your lecturer's face when they go to open the drawer and everything collapses around them.

ORDERING A PIZZA

- Tell the order taker a rival pizza place is on the other line and you're going with the lowest bidder.
- Give them your address and when they ask 'What do you want?' exclaim, 'Oh, just surprise me!' and hang up.
- Order a Big Mac Super-Value Meal.
- Answer their questions with questions.
- Tell them to put the crust on top this time.
- Do not name the toppings you want. Rather, spell them out.
- Stutter on the letter 'p'.
- Ask what the order taker is wearing.
- Say hello, act stunned for five seconds, then behave as if they called you.
- Tell the order taker you're depressed. Get him/her to cheer you up.
- Ask if you get to keep the pizza box. When they say yes, heave a sigh of relief.

- Put the accent on the last syllable of 'pepperoni'. Use the long 'i' sound.
- Amuse the order taker with little-known facts about country music.
- Ask to see a menu.
- Ask what their phone number is. Hang up, call them and ask again.
- Use expletives like 'Great Caesar's Ghost' and 'Jesus Joseph and Mary in Tinsel Town'.
- Ask for the guy who took your order last time.
- Ask if the pizza is organically grown.
- Learn to play a blues riff on the harmonica. Stop talking at regular intervals to play it.
- Make the first topping you order mushrooms. Make the last thing you say 'No mushrooms, please'. Hang up before they have a chance to respond.
- Haggle.

- Ask if it is possible to lease, rent or hire-purchase a pizza.
- Ask how many dolphins were killed to make that pizza.
- Ask how many trees were destroyed to make the cardboard box that the pizza will come in.
- Dance all around the word 'pizza'. Avoid saying it at all costs. If he/she says it, say, 'Please don't mention that word.'
- Order a steamed pizza.
- Terminate the call with, 'Remember, we never had this conversation.'

SOAP SUDS

Soap suds can be very funny things, particularly when there is vast quantities of them.

Use your imagination and have fun.

LOTSA SUDS

Recipe for large quantities of soapsuds:
Fill a large bucket with hot water.

Empty contents of one bottle of dishwashing detergent into bucket.

Drop in a few pounds of dry ice that has been crushed to small pieces.

Stand back!

Recipe will fill a phone booth or a small room (or even a big one).

Using the above recipe is a great trick to play in the back of a truck.

While you are stopped at traffic signals, the whole back area will fill up to the rim with suds.

Then, as you accelerate away from the lights, large chunks of suds will break loose and waft lazily through the air, causing much consternation to the traffic behind.

On the freeway the result will be just as good with much smaller pieces of suds billowing out of the back of the truck.

It will look like a snowstorm!

The soap can be omitted from the above recipe to obtain fog.

A phone booth that is opaque with dense fog looks pretty strange, as does your mate's bedroom.

SWARMING

Swarming—getting a big group of people together for a common, often crazy, purpose—is a new type of practical joke that is easy to organise because of the proliferation of mobile phones, text messages and the enthusiasm for people to get involved.

A large crowd of people can be organised in a small amount of time by sending text messages or emailing. They turn up at a given point, do some mindless thing or another and then disperse.

It can have amusing results.

Swarming began about ten years ago, with one of the first instances being in Washington. A group called Critical Mass would be organised by cell phone and text message to gather at a given point, at a given time— usually the first Friday of each month.

They would arrive on bicycles and clog Washington streets, protesting the effects of the automobile. They acted like a swarm of bees, changing direction as a group and at will.

'The people up front and the people in back are in constant communication, by cell phone and walkie-talkies and hand signals,' one of the organisers told *The Washington Post*.

'Everything is played by ear. On the fly, we can change the direction of the swarm—230 people, a giant bike mass. That's why the police have very little control. They have no idea where the group is going.'

POSSIBLE PRACTICAL JOKES USING THE SWARMING TECHNIQUE

Text friends and acquaintances to arrive at a given place at a given time and wait for a given signal to throw their jackets in the air and go 'Whoop!'

Then quietly disband.

The sight of a big group of people, who, for no cause, do this, is intriguing and puzzling for on-lookers.

Then, when the jacket-throwers just walk off, without a word to each other and go about their lives, it is even more perplexing for witnesses.

Text friends and acquaintances to arrive at a given place at a given time and wait for a given signal whereby everyone will perform a limp fall.

A limp fall is poetry in motion—being able to fall to the ground as if struck by lightning. No sound, little movement, just a graceful falling to the ground.

Stay prone for exactly two minutes.

Then, all as one, stand, dust yourselves off and disperse.

Text or email community and friends, turn up at a given place, at a given time and on a given signal sing a well-known song from *The Sound of Music*. For example, the one that starts, 'Doh a deer, a female deer.'

When the song is over and without further ado, disperse.

Text friends and acquaintances to arrive at a riverside or water feature in your area and, at a given time and a given signal, take off all your clothes and jump naked into the water.

Wait ten seconds, emerge from the water and without speaking or giving eye contact to anybody, dress and disperse.

Text friends and acquaintances to arrive at a certain shopping centre at a given time and wait for a given signal where everybody will go into the nearest shop, buy one item only and then disperse.

Text friends and acquaintances to arrive at a train station at a given time. Wait for a given signal and take the first train that comes along for one station only.

Alight.

Catch the next train back to where you came from.

Disperse.

TRICKS TO PLAY WITH DOORS

AWASH

Balance a nearly full bucket of water against someone's door at night.

When they open it the next morning it will fall and flood their room.

Even better against elevator doors.

WHERE'S THE DOORKNOB?

Remove someone's doorknob and reinstall it with the lock on the inside.

Works best if the victim is in the room and the door is locked and you have his/her keys.

WHERE'S THE DOOR?

Brick up the entrances to a building at night before anyone arrives. If the victim has a recessed door, fill the area flush with the wall (perhaps with drywall) and paint to match the wall.

The victim will return to a wall where the door used to be.

CAN'T GET IN THERE

Place clear tape across the outside of a door from top to bottom. Frequently people will run into it, especially if they are in a hurry.

WELDED IN

If the door is metal and has a metal frame, weld the person into (or out of) their room.

This trick can be done to the hinges as well if there is no metal door.

STEAL A PERSON'S DOOR

Unscrew the door from its hinges and take off with it and hide it. Have them running all over the place trying to find it.

The best thing is to have them end up finding it somewhere near where they started, like in the next room.

DOOR JAM

Jam so many coins as you can between the door and the door frame, that the person cannot turn the doorknob to get out.

Even better, if the coins are super glued in place to prevent removal.

STICKY

Put Vaseline on the inside doorknob to prevent them from being able to turn the knob.

PEEPHOLE

Reverse the peephole on the people's door.
Allows for some interesting spying, since very few people actually check this part of the door.